Quiet Time with God

Quiet Time with God

Kristen Johnson Ingram

Judson Press ® Valley Forge

QUIET TIME WITH GOD

Copyright © 1984
Judson Press, Valley Forge, PA 19482-0851

Unless otherwise indicated, the Scripture quotations in this publication are from the Revised Standard Version of the Bible copyrighted 1946, 1952 © 1971, 1973 by the Division of Christian Education of the National Council of the Churches of Christ in the U.S.A., and used by permission

Other quotations of the Bible are from *The New English Bible,* Copyright © The Delegates of the Oxford University Press and The Syndics of the Cambridge University Press 1961, 1970.

Library of Congress Cataloging in Publication Data
Ingram, Kristen J.
  Quiet time with God.
  Includes bibliographical references.
  1. Prayer.   2. Spiritual life.   I. Title.
BV210.2.I54   1984   248.3   83-24856
ISBN 0-8170-1026-2

Contents

Preface

"Your telephone has been busy for a half hour," said my friend accusingly, standing at my front door.

"I was meditating," I told her and invited her to come in. "I took my phone off the hook."

She almost ran away. To her, words like "meditate" connoted Transcendental Meditation, "mysticism" meant psychic phenomena and possibly spiritualism, and the mention of a book by a monk brought forth a verbal spew of disgust about "medieval fanaticism."

She was persuaded to stay, partly because she needed my help on a community project and partly because she was a member of the Sunday school class for adults that I teach. She hadn't heard anything she could directly identify as heresy; so I gave her a cup of coffee and began to explain my solitary inner life of worship and prayer to her.

At the end of an hour, she wailed, "Why doesn't anyone ever help us Protestants to understand this?"

Someone is going to try to do just that—in this book.

1

Seeking the Holy

... and he went out to the mountain to pray ... (Luke 6:12)

There is a place beyond worldly care or involvement. It is a place of utter silence, a time and space infinitely proportioned, where we can enter into a holy and intimate relationship with God, leaving the world and its glittering wares behind.

That place is the kingdom of heaven, and we reach it through the veil within us.

We must seek the lost arts of meditation and contemplation if we are to see the face of God as God wishes to present it—within the holiest of holy places. Just as the tabernacle of the nomadic Jews was a model of something heavenly, so it is also a model of the inner person that is within us.

Beyond the veil of the temple or tabernacle was a place of particular grace and blessing, where only the high priest could enter and make atonement at a certain time of year. But when Christ made his full, perfect, and sufficient sacrifice, that veil was torn in two, and we became a royal priesthood.

There is still a "veil" in our inner temple. The rational mind and the demands of the world tend to veil the innermost holy place. It is not all bad, this covering of our sanctification; we do not wish to expose the holiest things of God to a swinish world.

On the other hand, we must not veil from ourselves the inner life that holds Christ's presence. We are the high priests in our own temples; no one else but God can enter into our most secret prayer life.

The holy place is not a hiding place; it is, in spite of its timeless and spaceless character, the location of our motivation to action, of the refinement and direction of our passions, and of the restructuring of our conscious lives. The spirit within us is neither a frivolous appendage to body and mind nor a lovely and ethereal bit of heaven imprisoned in "low" flesh. What we seek in the life of mystical prayer is *transformation* in all areas of life.

To approach God in the contemplative manner is to discard the rational temporarily, so that when the reason of our faith and action is taken up again, it has begun a process of transmutation. What God wants is a holy and set-apart people; but all too often we try through rational means to make ourselves holy from the outside in, rather than seeking our sanctification within and then letting that spirituality pervade all areas of our lives.

Discipline, petitionary prayer, reading, and travail before the Lord may be nearly worthless until we begin to let the spirit within us bubble as a spring, flowing over our lives and occupations and ideas. The great saints of Christendom did not take up, say, poverty or chastity or self-denial to *become* holy; rather, they did it because the holiness within was pressing outward, demanding refinement of mind and conscious thought, of physical body, of speech and eating habits and use of the world's currency.

"You shall be holy unto me, for I, the LORD, am holy," said God to the people more than once in the Old Testament. Did that mean that they were to try their very best to act right so that they could get good marks from God? Or did it, more likely, imply that, given the opportunity, God would make them a consecrated people from within, while they tried to avoid getting caught in the snarls of worldly existence?

There is something in us that constantly impels us to action. Good! Without action no good works would be done in the name of Jesus. The widows and orphans would starve and prisoners would go unvisited if we did nothing but lapse inward.

The trouble is, most of us have let that action-impeller take over. We do, we figure, we plan, and we think. Most of us only let the nonrational take over in our dreams, and we're usually not in very good touch with those dream experiences.

There is, however latent, however dormant, a nonthinking, nonrational, side to all of us. In a moment we can be transfixed by the glory and simplicity of a golden poppy. We may know no botany; we may be unable to name the flower parts or identify the flower beyond calling it a poppy. Yet somehow there is a moment of relationship. We know not, for a moment, where "we" stop and the flower begins. There is no analysis, even, of our feelings. It is not a case of our inner voice saying, "Here is a person looking at a flower and enjoying it." For a moment, like the poppy, we just *are*.

This side of us can be called upon, taught, nurtured, and brought into an adoring, intimate relationship with God. This is the self that doesn't even know how to pray but allows the Spirit to plead for it, with utterances beyond words (see Romans 8:26).

Now, through contemplative prayer, each busy, active mind can be trained to allow its intuitive or receptive side to transcend that endless, merciless progression of constant reasoning.

The ancient Chinese called the two sides of nature, including the sides of human nature, "yang" and "yin". Although they did not conceive of the nature of the one God and had to function without even a promise of Christ, the Chinese philosophers did have some valuable insights and did discover some excellent mechanical and physical principles. Though they made errors in their approach to God and proposed some philosophical principles that do not fit the Christian's life, they did recognize the polarity of nature.

Yang and yin are simply names for the opposite but complementary principles that prevail in nature. Physicists excite us at the outer edge of mystery by describing the affective behavior of protons and electrons; magnets demonstrate the power of positive and negative energies. Our car batteries have plus and minus signs on their poles.

Now, psychobiologists have investigated, to the philosophers' delight, the left and right sides of the brain. Yang-yin, north-south, left-right, plus-minus, male-female—all these factors function in nature, clear to the very structure of the human thinking organ.

We are, largely, a right-handed world. The right hand is controlled by the left side of the brain, and vice versa. Right-handedness, "maleness," thinking, figuring, mechanizing, doing—all these are on that left side of the brain. So are the major speech centers for right-handed people.

The right side of the brain (or "left hand") is the receptive, intuitive, "female," sensitive, and responsive center of both conscious and unconscious thought.

"This is a coffee cup," says my left brain, making a quick assessment of an object that I see. "I love it. I could plant flowers in it," says my right brain intuitively.

"I have deduced logically that there is a God," says my "right hand," and it sets about writing a systematic theology. Wordless, awed, and in love with God, my "left hand" simply adores God in receptive meditation.

Thus, we see ourselves in a kind of Martha-Mary juxtaposition to our own spirit. "Work," says Martha; "Receive," says Mary, at God's feet.

Like Paul, we are likely at this point to cry out, as he did at the snarl he described in the seventh chapter of Romans, "Miserable creature that I am! Who will deliver me from this terrible paradox?" (Romans 7:24, author's paraphrase).

Christ, able and ready and desirous and jealous, is able to deliver us. He wants all of us, in every way, and is offering himself to our own growth and salvation, through that inner door to the kingdom.

And we are able to "work out (our) own salvation in fear and trembling" (Philippians 2:12). With the awe due God for the creation of our entire person and with the reverence due that holy of holies within, we may push open the door *from the inside* simply by directing our thought into patterns of meditation. As we do this mighty miracle, the "left hand," which has been so neglected, begins to function.

The "left hand," or right side of the brain if you prefer to stay scientifically oriented, is the most neglected member of the human organism. In the rush of our culture to accomplish great mathematical, scientific, financial, pyschological, and theological things, we have let our nonrational, receptive side go to the nether regions in the proverbial handbasket.

We have invented incredible computers—and we are lacking in imagination. We cure diseases—and we forget to heal. We hold classes on marriage—and we neglect love. Worst of all, we preach, pray, intercede, and liturgize, while ignoring the sweet voice of God speaking to our inner beings. No wonder we have moral decay in the midst of technological achievement. There is no chance for transfiguration because a rational world cannot even imagine such a thing!

"You must therefore be mentally stripped for action," says Peter in his First Epistle, "perfectly self-controlled" (1 Peter 1:13, NEB). For years, I saw this passage as a demand on my own self-restraint, a call to some kind of spiritual gymnastics program in which, by sheer force of will, I would learn to avoid overeating, feeling annoyed, and being upset about anything.

But "stripped for action" brings a picture to my mind of my running days. I would enter the school gym and take off all my street clothing, rub myself down with a damp towel, and put on an outfit of light clothing and cloth shoes. What for? To be bound in, restrained? No, rather, to be freed to run.

My whole day would melt behind me. The difficult geometry lesson, the argument with my parents, the library assignment, the worry about my boyfriend's behavior—all would fly from my mind as I pursued a totally pleasurable, nonrational activity.

I would run like the wind, around and around that track, until I fell with joyous exhaustion.

And what about that "perfectly self-controlled" part? Well, that certainly did not restrain me. When an athlete controls his or her body, or a driver controls a car, he or she *directs* it. With almost no conscious thought, I stripped off my heavy everyday clothing and directed my body to greater freedom and a deeper connection with its needs and abilities.

In the same way we can let the intellect strip itself for the action of mystical contemplation by letting it teach itself perfect control and self-direction.

Peter continues:

> Fix your hopes on the gift of grace which is to be yours when Jesus Christ is revealed. As obedient children, do not let your characters be shaped any longer by the desires you cherished in your days of ignorance. The One who called you is holy; like him, be holy in all your behaviour, because the Scripture says, 'You shall be holy, for I am holy' (1 Peter 1:13-16, NEB).

As we learn to meditate—to pray with the heart rather than with the mind—we fix our hope on God's mercy and grace. We also fix our thoughts in a way that is, perhaps, new and different but peaceful and refining. And our behavior is shaped by the new knowledge we gain—knowledge that, for once, is not based on "input material" from outside us. The "left hand," the dreamer, feeds the rational with the presence of God, and we are made holy.

That which can be known cannot be learned—but it can be practiced. The holy place cannot be described—but it can be experienced and lived in.

This is mysticism.

2

Centering

Back in my running days, before I became a doting grandmother, I was called upon always to maintain a perfect balance between tension and relaxation when I ran. Now I realize that without some tension I would barely be able to walk—I would probably sleep—and without relaxation, exercise would leave my body in a mass of knots.

Runners, gymnasts, and dancers can all tell us about the process of establishing this perfect tensional balance. When they begin training, there seems to be a time of getting in touch with the body itself and its sensations of location and balance (or of dislocation and imbalance). They look within themselves to the spot that communicates, "On the level," or "Too much weight on the right leg," much as a spirit level indicates to a carpenter when a board is flat.

Later, as the athletes begin to direct their bodies successfully, they discover that there is a "route" through some heretofore unexplored part of the brain. Something beyond consciousness, an "inner director," takes over. The body's natural pain killers begin to produce euphoria in runners or others who press toward a mark of physical exertion. That which was painful or difficult becomes easy and fun. Some athletes even use a word or phrase to get in touch with this "inner director." I can remember murmuring, "Cen-ter-ing, cen-ter-ing," and feeling my legs and arms—in fact my whole being—respond with strength and direction.

The spiritual process is not so different from this. Prayer becomes effective when it is used as a centering or balancing device to make us grow and to make us spiritually available to God. A perfect balance is created between speaking and listening, giving and receiving, between relaxation into God's presence and alertness to God's direction. Ancient Greek and Russian Orthodox church fathers called this balancing process "putting the mind in the heart." Having released the left hand from its shackle, we let it open the gate of the heart and pour the mind into it.

If I were to go to, say, Japan, and ask to be taught to meditate in a Zen monastery, I would be told to sit in a certain way, think a certain thought, and so forth. For some reason, many Christians balk at telling one another how to meditate in the presence of Jesus Christ.

The author of *The Cloud of Unknowing,* who lived in England in the fourteenth century, says, "This is what you are to do: lift your heart up to the Lord with a gentle stirring of love desiring him for his own sake, and not for his gifts. . . . And so diligently persevere until you feel joy in it."[1]

He suggests that we keep our syllables of prayer to one, inwardly repeating the word "God . . . God . . ." until we are saying it with the same intensity as "Help!" or "Fire!"[2]

Many people enjoy this one-syllable dialogue with God. Others prefer to use a longer prayer of the heart. Some use the "Jesus Prayer" found in Mark's Gospel (10:47) and developed by Russian Orthodox pilgrims: "Lord Jesus Christ, Son of God, have mercy on me, a sinner."

Frequently, that prayer is shortened to "Lord Jesus Christ, have mercy on me!" The results in a life of constantly using this prayer are found in a small book called *The Way of the Pilgrim,* written by an unknown Russian of the last century.[3]

Some modern contemplatives prefer to write their own "centering prayer" or prayer of the heart. Like the Jesus Prayer, it contains an adoration (the use of one of the names of God) and a petition. Although many people prefer simply to use the name of God or to think, *Jesus ... Jesus ... Jesus,* in their period of meditation, others prefer to create a simple prayer of the heart for centering. An example of a centering prayer might be "God, let me know your love." Perhaps another would be "Jesus, please walk beside me" or "Jesus, fill me with your love." Ask God for whatever will bring you to wholeness and readiness for a complete Christian life.

This little prayer is used during daily mediation time, as well as running like a murmuring stream through the heart all day. (In fact, I have come to the place where, if I waken at night, my centering prayer is on my lips, apparently "saying itself" in my sleep.) Ron DelBene, an Episcopal minister, has conducted seminars throughout the country, teaching clergy and lay people to write and use what he calls "breath prayers." His book *The Breath of Life* describes the method he uses in helping people find their heartfelt petitions.[4]

Here the puritan ethic raises its head. "All this sounds selfish," someone says. "Is it right to be constantly petitioning God that way?"

One night at one of our parish meditation classes, Patty, one of the students who was having great difficulty after two weeks of contemplative prayer, raised these concerns almost exactly.

"Patty, I'm cold," I said, "Would you let me use your coat?"

She was wearing a pantsuit with a knit top. She looked at me, puzzled, and I asked her again. Finally, she said, "You could certainly wear my coat, but I don't have one here."

The class members smiled. They saw what was coming.

"Well, then," one of the men burst in before I could go on, "how are you going to give the world anything until you have plenty of it inside?"

I might not have phrased it that way, but his forthright expression was a perfect answer to her concerns. Until we are filled, we are not as useful to our brothers and sisters in the world as we might be. Our "link" with God is not complete.

You may choose one syllable or seven to call on God. Close your eyes, sit comfortably, with your spine upright, and then let God put your centering prayer into your heart. Think of yourself as a bell, tuned to a certain note; when correctly struck, the bell will create beauty and will function properly. In contemplation, when God rings us like a bell, we know we are one with God. We are functioning as created persons in the world and yet are in perfect union with the Almighty.

Stay with the prayer in silence perhaps five minutes. I use a calculator with a soft "beep" to end my prayer time; I started with the timer on the kitchen stove, but after a few close calls with heart failure at the loud buzz, I bought a gentler timer.

This timing is important. It is part of our discipline. Many people need discipline to start something, but they don't realize that good self-control means stopping prayer, too. Timing will also keep our minds from wandering, creating irrelevant images, or putting us to sleep.

If the mind does wander, bring it back gently and lovingly to the word(s) of your centering prayer. When your time is up, say the Lord's Prayer and give thanks for your time together.

Once you have arrived at the words of your centering prayer and have set a time each day for meditation, think about creating a place. I usually go to the deep rocking chair in the living room just before I eat breakfast. Sometimes I take a picture of Jesus to look at for a moment as inspiration. Other days I just look out the window at a flowerbed or the willow tree or the wonderful Oregon hillsides before I close my eyes. Whatever puts us in touch with God is what we can concentrate on for a minute; then it is helpful to read a line or two of Scripture or to whisper aloud a memorized line from the Bible.

This is not the time for Bible study; we need to set aside a separate time of day for our intercessory prayers and for our study of God's Word. This is a time set apart for relationship with Christ, not for work of any kind.

Many people like to wash their hands or take their daily shower just before meditation. This simple act can remind us of our baptism and of the miracle of God's redemptive love for us in and through Jesus Christ. Bringing this frame of mind to the place of meditation will propel us more quickly into the "tabernacle state," in which we begin to function in holiness.

There are days when the centering is effective but there are also days when our concentration is nonexistent. These are the times to wait patiently, to rest in the Lord. Poor concentration is not necessarily an indication of low spirituality. It is more likely to be a result of unusual stress, poor diet, lack of rest, or temporary inability to "draw the curtains" and cut off our worldly cares.

As we journey into God's kingdom in silent prayer, we discover that there are stages. At first, in meditation we are *thinking* our centering prayer; later, we begin simply to have it inside, especially if we keep the word going all day as we work and act. In the third stage or prayer, our word stops. Conscious prayer stops. And we find ourselves in wordless, joyful adoration, in perfect communion with our Lord. This is contemplation.

As lovers often simply hold hands and gaze wordlessly into each other's eyes, so contemplatives find themselves in a love relationship, perfectly aware and yet separated from everything else—even their own words of prayer!

It sometimes takes a while to achieve that level of contemplation, simply because most of us are too out of shape spiritually to invite that state of being. But it will come if we reach and if we allow ourselves to be loved by God.

"Strive and strive and strive," cried Teresa of Avila in the fourteenth century; "we were made for nothing else."[5]

This medieval nun founded the Carmelite order, establishing convents throughout southeastern Europe. She was, however, scarcely an other-worldly woman, in spite of her mysticism and her vows. She was outspoken with kings and princes, apparently losing all fear of earthly retribution and all desire to curry the favor of men as she came closer and closer to Christ.

Likewise, she was outspoken with God, because they knew

and loved each other. There is a story that once, while she was traveling on business for her order, the wheels of her carriage stuck in heavy mud. Getting out to help push, she shook her fist at heaven.

"If this is the way You treat your friends, no wonder You have so few," she railed, perfectly at ease with God.

There is a fourth stage of prayer—and a fourth way of being— that not all Christians care to pursue. The English author of *The Cloud of Unknowing* calls this phase "Perfect."[6] Mystics of the Western tradition usually call it "Union."

It is a phase of prayer that is, traditionally, right under our noses but missed because of its deep demands on each individual. One does not enter into the holy of holies easily. To reach for union with God, for total accord, or for a life in the divine Person requires that we drop everything we believe about God and ourselves and let God scoop us up.

This is a kind of *parousia*. It means that we scrape away or even destroy our images and concepts of God and let ourselves be taken into God.

Grace is always a risky business, and while no kind of prayer will leave us unchanged, to risk union with God is to risk having one's entire being transmuted.

"Prayer is photosynthesis of the soul," rejoiced Carolyn Rhea, a Baptist laywoman who wrote articulately about her own prayer life.[7] Indeed, the "substance" of God changes within us in much the same way as light and chlorophyll interact to promote the formation of carbohydrates. In this phase we breathe God in and out in the same yielding and nonrational way that a plant exchanges its oxygen for carbon dioxide.

At this point, I again hear the voice of my puritan friend. Schooled in the Reformation, he or she is wary of anything "not contained in the Bible." I would comfort this fundamentalist with all my heart and remind him or her that the Spirit will lead us in all truth.

The Protestant apologist A. W. Tozer writes:

The Bible will never be a living Book to us until we are convinced that God is articulate in His universe. To jump from a dead, impersonal world to a dogmatic Bible is too much for most people. They may admit that they *should* accept the Bible as the Word of God, and they may try to think of it as such, but they find it impossible to believe that the words there on the page are actually for them. A man may *say*, "These words are addressed to me," and yet in his heart not feel and know that they are. He is the victim of a divided psychology. He tries to think of God as mute everywhere else and vocal only in a book.[8]

Tozer, like Augustine, Thomas à Kempis, John Wesley, and Thomas Merton, knows that the Word of God spoke the world into being, called to Abraham and Moses, summoned the child Samuel from his bed, and has drawn dreamers and mystics to God's feet throughout time. The Word of God did not begin or cease with the writing of Scripture; God is not, and never has been, silent. God is speaking to us right now.

"When in former times God spoke to our forefathers, he spoke in fragmentary and varied fashion through the prophets," says Hebrews 1:1 (NEB). "But in this the final age he has spoken to us in the Son whom he has made heir ..." (1:2, NEB). "'Today if you hear his voice, do not grow stubborn as in those days of rebellion at that time of testing in the desert. ... I said, Their hearts are forever astray; they would not discern my ways; as I vowed in my anger, they shall never enter my rest'" (Hebrews 3:7-11, NEB).

In order to "enter [his] rest," we must listen and respond to our Lord. To become one *with* Christ is to become one *like* him: a perfect, balanced response to the Word of God. God speaks the Word; Christ becomes the Word. (There may be some Christological heresy in this sentence since it implies a time when Christ was *not*. The Word existed in the beginning, with God and as God. But Christ's perfect response to God's will and his complete willingness to operate in God's love are earthly manifestations of Christ as the Word becoming flesh.)

Jesus asks us to dwell in him and to let him dwell in us. To make this command a reality, we must constantly open ourselves, more and more, until we are full of God; we must seek more and more to find the presence of God and bury ourselves in God's bosom.

Once, at a retreat in the Idaho woods, I went for a walk alone, to relax and reflect. I sat down on a log near a greater patch of purple pasqueflowers, with their deep throats and whiskery orifices.

An immense bumblebee flew into sight and lighted on a stem; he investigated the flower and suddenly, as if he were not one of the clumsiest of God's insect creatures, rose an inch from the plant, drew back, and hurled himself into the hidden center of the flower. He may still be in there, taking nectar, ecstatic.

I was transported. My most eloquent prayers to that date had been trash, words, nothing. That furry bee had demonstrated to me what real prayer was about—hurling ourselves with abandon into the heart of God.

3

Write These Words

You shall take these words of mine to heart and keep them in mind;
you shall bind them as a sign on the hand and wear them as a
phylactery on the forehead. Teach them to your children, and speak
of them indoors and out of doors, when you lie down and when you
rise. Write them on the doorposts of your houses and on your gates.
Then you will live long . . . in the land which the LORD swore to your
forefathers to give them, for as long as the heavens are above the
earth. (Deuteronomy 11:18-21, NEB)

Recently I went to a gift shop to buy a present for a thirteen-year-old girl. As I wandered through the blown-glass
animals, gift books, wind chimes, and jewelry, my eye
fell on a beautiful red-leather five-year diary. I picked it up,
opened the tiny lock to look inside, and was almost overwhelmed by a sense of terrible heaviness and wrongdoing.

The sensation persisted. Terrible waves of ancient guilt
seemed to wash over me, and I quickly put the book down,
walked outside, and sat in my car, wondering what was going
on inside me.

Suddenly, I saw a picture of myself at about twelve. My Aunt
Betty, a vivacious and brilliant woman whom I adored, was
giving me a Christmas gift. It was, indeed, a red-leather diary.

"You'll enjoy this," she said, and it sounded like a command
from God.

For a few weeks I wrote eagerly, even splashing into next

year's writing area. Then I wrote cheerfully but with less delight for a few more weeks. My mother, a professional writer, would remark, "I'm glad you're keeping a journal. It will help you in your other writing." So, with renewed zeal, I continued to jot down my days and thoughts.

But soon my entries became more sporadic. During the spring term at school, a thirteen-year-old boy began to pay some attention to me.

Eventually I quit writing. The red leather gleamed in the light of my bedside table, reminding me of my lack of self-discipline. I moved it to a shelf and finally to the bottom of a dresser drawer, feeling as though I had failed Aunt Betty, myself, and in all probability, God.

The evening after I caught this memory, I shared my experience with a meditation class I was leading in my church. The others began to nod in assent; one woman had tears in her eyes, and another student, an older man, cried, "It's as if we all plot to make ourselves feel guilty and inadequate."

Indeed, it does seem that way, and we have help. It is no accident that one Old Testament translation of Satan's name is "The Accuser." We are constantly upbraiding ourselves, with all the aid hell can muster, to feel guilty because we aren't staying on diets, writing journals, exercising, walking a mile daily, calling our parents, keeping up correspondence, and, in general, doing more than is possible.

Although many of us have guilt-tainted memories of journal keeping, it may come as a surprise that I tell students of contemplation, "Keep a spiritual journal." Don't set unattainable goals and don't feel guilty if you skip a day or so, but do try to write after every meditation period.

The spiritual journal is not to be a recitation of the day's activities nor a place to remind yourself of upcoming obligations. You have a calendar or desk book for that. Neither is the journal to be a cathartic outpouring of every possible thought. Although such an outpouring might be psychologically beneficial, we are seeking another set of goals through the writing of the spiritual journal.

First, if we follow each period of meditation with a brief journal entry—say, two sentences at first—we can soon chart our own growth in prayer. Whatever happens, we write it down: "Today, I found myself concentrating on the beauty of Christ as I prayed. The time went quickly," tells us something different from the frustrating days when we write, "Many thoughts and ideas kept rushing in. I was restless and had to keep bringing my mind back to prayer."

Do we need to look at our own progress? Is it somehow "unspiritual" to measure one's own prayer growth? If so, then Paul was unspiritual when he said,

> When I was a child, my speech, my outlook, and my thoughts were all childish. When I grew up, I had finished with childish things. Now we see only puzzling reflections in the mirror, but then we shall see face to face. *My knowledge is now partial; then it will be whole, like God's knowledge of me* (1 Corinthians 13:12-13, NEB; author's emphasis).

At one moment one is spiritually a child; then an adolescent; and so on, until, with the aid of the mental mirror in our journals, we can begin to see ourselves *as God sees us.* Paul, in his first address to the confused Corinthian church, charted his own progress as a son of the royal household, admitting that at some moments his understanding even of himself was incomplete, but he strove to see himself as Christ saw him.

Paul of course strove for more than identity and self-understanding. He pressed forward toward the mark constantly, yearning to be what God wanted him to be. This brings us to a second reason for keeping a journal: learning to see areas of spiritual life that are undeveloped.

It frequently becomes apparent to me that I have achieved an unbalanced spirituality. Perhaps I wax in prayer but lack understanding of God's plan for my work. Or I may feel inclined toward a kind of spirituality that is more intellectual than God wants. Perhaps at times my self-discipline is admirable, but I feel as dry as the desert in my prayer life. All of these things are recorded; and like a tree that is overgrown on one side and spindly on the other, I can submit myself to God's pruning.

Those who have grown grapes know that only new growth will bear fruit. Thus a fairly severe pruning and cutting is required every year if we are eager for a pantry full of grape jam next winter. We must watch closely to see where we are *not* fruitful and ask God to help us with God's sometimes severe mercy.

It is usually after a scrupulous rereading of my journal that I go to see my pastor for spiritual direction. Most contemplative Christians find it helpful to find someone—a minister, a church school teacher, or a layperson of deep spiritual wisdom—who would be willing to give regular spiritual direction. This is not to be confused with pastoral counseling, which usually deals with emotional or psychological situations or with family problems. Spiritual direction is *not* psychological advice.

Many times we have a third reason for keeping a journal. In the journal, we can make a word-offering to God that is perhaps different from those in our prayers. God loves us and pleads for our love in return; our journal writing is one opportunity for us to offer our love to God.

Many who come to meditation classes say, "I want to know God's will for me."

"Splendid!" I always say. "I know God's will. God *yearns* for you. God's will is to have your love, the love of the bride that the church is meant to be."

Think of the church. Close your eyes, and see yourself merging with a huge body of people; now see that body transformed into the bride of Christ, wearing a simple linen garment, running to meet her loved one. This is God's will and desire for everyone who has come to Christ: that we come as an eager and purified bride, with words of love on our lips.

When we write in our journals, we can place on paper the words that our lips have not formed. We can thank God for our creation, for our sustenance, and for all the blessings of life. We can be thankful for Jesus, our brother, our high priest, through whose broken body we may enter the holy place as a Levitical high priest entered through a veil. We can thank God

for the Holy Spirit, whose work in us as teacher and strength-
ener continues, day by day, and who is earnest for our salvation.

To write in our journal is to love Jesus in words. He wants
our wholeness so desperately that he was willing to die a
shameful death, and now we have a chance to write our loving
thanks.

There is a final reason for the journal, and that is to hear
God speak. A. W. Tozer, the preacher and teacher who drank
at the wells of the Christian mystics, reminds us that God's
voice did not begin and end with the writing of Scripture.[1] God
has always spoken and speaks still. God's Word of creation
rings in us as a carefully tuned bell rings at its maker's touch.

Usually, we "hear" God in prayer by receiving direction or
help in response to our petitions. Or sometimes after we ask
for such aid, God speaks or acts through another person. We
pray for a word of comfort, and then a friend rings the doorbell.
We wonder if we should move to another state, and later we
hear someone discussing that very place at a party. It happens
to all of us all the time.

For the contemplative Christian, the Word of God is not
limited to Scripture, nor does it simply mean the metaphorical
word of creation. The Word that spoke us into being also speaks
us into love, action, faith, and adventure; and many times God's
Word to us flows into our journal writing.

Only a few days ago, in preparation for writing this chapter,
I leafed through some of my old prayer journals. Most had a
few sentences written after each prayer time, twice daily, plus
any other remarks I wanted to make before I went to bed. My
eyes fell on an entry written several years ago, in which I described God's throne and my relationship to it. Jesus' words
to Peter were renewed in my mind as I read the entry. "You did
not learn that from mortal man"(Matthew 16:17). As I looked
at my handwriting, at words I scarcely knew, I knew that mortals
had not taught me a single phrase of that day's entry. God had
spoken to me in prayer and into my journal in a life-changing

way. Of this I am sure because the date of that entry fell at a time when, after great tragedy for a family member, I was struggling with anger and wavering faith. From that date forward, the struggle stopped.

I wrote God's words in my journal; they were recorded and bound on my wrists and round my brain as "phylacteries" for thought. I keep them on the doorposts and gates of my heart, and my days in God's land are long and meaningful.

"But," I can hear someone cry, "as wonderful as that is, what about the days we miss? What if we forget to write, or even skip a day of silent prayer? Aren't we back to the five-year-diary? Isn't it just another case of turning in homework?"

First, the journal is a blessing to us, not a duty. The more we write, the more we find ourselves writing. It's fun. But everyone, including the modern-day monk Thomas Merton, who left his own journals for the hungry, did not write every day. Sometimes you are up all night with a croupy baby or rushing to catch a plane on business. Some days you just plain forget. It isn't necessary to psychoanalyze yourself looking for a "deep" reason. If you miss a day, or a week, write again another time. Writing is a gift, not a chore.

Second, the journal is intensely personal, between you and God. Submit your journal to God, and God will take authority over it. When we make a true offering, God always multiplies it. God told the Israelites that, as they set up cities of sanctuary, their borders would be extended. As their borders were extended, God promised to increase their cities of sanctuary. Mercy and love give rise to growth, and growth to more mercy and love. If we jot a few words in a notebook that is dedicated to the love of our Lord Jesus Christ, he will bless those words and "extend the borders" of our ability to write.

The journal is private. The only person who might read any of it is one who is giving spiritual direction. It is not to be shared with other family members because it is part of your covenant relationship with God.

When do we write? Always after prayer or when we've had

a powerful dream (much more of that later). Often, we write when we can take a moment to reflect before retiring at night or whenever we feel the need to record something about our Christ life. Many people like to record a few words after studying Scripture, especially if the study spoke to them particularly that day.

Whether we use a spiral notebook or a monogrammed leather one, the journal should be on the shelf near our Bible and whatever other books of inspiration we use. Don't let "The Accuser" push you into hiding it in your dresser drawer!

4

The Visitation of the Magi:
God's Gift of Dreams

How silently, how silently The wondrous gift is given!
  So God imparts to human hearts The blessings of his heaven.
No ear may hear his coming, But in this world of sin,
  Where meek souls will receive him, still The dear Christ enters in.

(O Little Town of Bethlehem; Phillips Brooks, 1868)

The wise men came through the desert, following a star and bearing rich and exotic gifts for the Child and his family. "Who sent you to bring these gifts?" the young mother might have asked; and one might imagine their answer: "We were sent by your own God."

In this single event the whole world had received the greatest gift of all history; God had become a child, lying in the straw. In Christ, God had "broken through" to confront men and women directly, and when Christ returned to heaven, we were left another gift, in the person of the Holy Spirit, who indwells all Christians.

God still breaks through to our human hearts "where meek souls will receive him," as the Christmas carol suggests. In our encounters with the living God, that "meekness" means willingness to receive and respond. It means *trust*. If we trust God with our waking moments, then we can ask God to occupy those hours during which we sleep, as well.

31

When Christians begin to use centering prayer as part of the spiritual pilgrimage, they usually find that the direction of their dreaming changes. They find that their dreams, like the rest of their nonrational activity, begin to be increasingly important.

Dreams *can* be injections of ideas from our psyches, or inner selves, bearing significant content from our own physical and emotional lives. Behavioral scientists have known for some time that dream life frequently is an accurate reflection of psychological growth.

Dreams can also be gifts from God. Every Christian is indwelt by the Holy Spirit and given spiritual discernment. If we record our dreams and offer them up in prayer, God will graciously give us insight into their meanings. We do not need the popular "dream books" that the world's marketplace offers. Instead, we should turn to God with every dream, whether it is pleasant or troublesome, asking for guidance.

In his First Epistle to the Corinthians, Paul reminds us that

> we have received not the spirit of the world, but the Spirit which is from God. . . . And we impart this in words not taught by human wisdom but taught by the Spirit, interpreting spiritual truths. . . .
>
> The unspiritual man does not receive the gifts of the Spirit of God, for they are folly to him, and he is not able to understand them because they are spiritually discerned. . . . But we have the mind of Christ (1 Corinthians 2:12-16).

"Doesn't interpretation of dreams belong to God?" asked Joseph, who became great in Egypt after he revealed the nature of Pharaoh's dream. And Daniel asked God to enable him not only to interpret Nebuchadnezzar's dream but to remember the dream itself, since the Babylonian ruler had forgotten it!

In each of these cases, God was faithful. Over and over, throughout both Old and New Testaments, God sent messages through dreams. In fact, the first two chapters of Matthew's Gospel, where the account of the Nativity is given, no less than *five* dreams are recorded as being critical to the situation. And for all these dreams, no "meaning" is left un-given.

The best way to interpret dreams is to assume that *all* people and/or animals (and, sometimes, even objects) in our dreams are aspects of ourselves. If I dream of being, say, at a party or a meeting, all the people there are parts of my personality or aspects of my spiritual life.

Our dreams are not to be viewed as predictors of the future. Many people are upset by occasional terrifying more-real-than-life dreams, and they wonder if these dreams are portents of a dire future. We must remember two facts: *one*, dreams are given to us as tools of insight for our own lives; and *two*, Christians do not meddle in the occult. There is a powerful biblical injunction against "divining," or trying to foretell the future. As a holy and separated people we must heed this rule. Therefore, we don't look at a dream as having an objective meaning or a message for someone else. Instead, we view dreams subjectively, as pictures of our own inner lives.

Sometimes, these gifts of the Magi are more abrasive in our lives than pleasurable. When I first began to pursue a deeper relationship with Christ, I had a series of dreams in which I was drowning, as, indeed, I was. We don't immerse ourselves in the untamed love of God without dying to self! I used the content of these dreams as a directive to prayer, asking to be shown where or how I was "fighting to stay alive"—that is, resisting God. I began a habit of examining my conscience for those subtle forms of arrogance and resistance that can lurk in the darker corners of my soul.

One woman in our parish, a Christian since childhood, had begun to read her Bible and attend church with renewed zeal after starting our meditation class. She dreamed one night that she could fly. Hers was not high-altitude flight; in fact, she was hovering about five feet above ground beside two friends who were walking along the road. Several times, she invited them to try flying, too, but one scoffed and said her ideas were childish. The other, pretending not to see her, read a thick book.

When she awoke, she at first felt exultant, but sorry for her two friends (members of her church) who in real life had said that they didn't want to find any deeper relationship with Christ than they had already experienced. My friend was on the verge of writing one of them a letter when she suddenly realized that this dream was not about her friends but about herself!

In spite of her renewed love for God, a side of her personality still scoffed at the childlike attitude necessary to be available to God; another aspect of her personality wanted to retreat into the intellectual, leaving prayer and the church behind. Taking the dream as a warning that all was not perfect in her own soul, she forgot about "zeal," especially toward others, and began to concentrate on loving God; soon, the dreams began to be of a different nature.

Scientific studies have shown that unless we record a dream or tell it to someone else within a few moments, we will probably forget it. The individual who claims that he or she "never dreams" *does* dream; he or she sleeps deeply and just never wakens enough to remember them.

I have read many books that instruct me to keep a note pad by the bedside and wake up to jot down every dream. Frankly, since I maintain a fairly high level of activity, I value a good night's sleep almost as much as I do my inner life! So I prefer to write down only those dreams which seem unusually clear or leave a vivid impression of spiritual content. Students of meditation may make their own choices in this matter.

According to physicians who study sleeping and dreaming patterns, our longest and most intense dreams are at the end of sleep, close to waking time. Perhaps it is another case of Jesus saving the best wine until last. In any event, this phenomenon makes these early-morning dreams easier to remember. It is good to share one's dreams at breakfast; we often recall details in the telling.

If I wake up in the middle of the night after a bad dream, I usually pray about it immediately and take a quick, sleepy look at the images of the dream. Why? Partly to help me remember the dream and partly to rob it of its power to frighten or upset me the next day.

The Rev. Morton Kelsey, author of several books on the inner spiritual life, including *Dreams: a Way to Listen to God*, suggests that the good and evil we encounter in dreams are purer than the good and evil of which we are aware when we are awake.[1] I can testify to this; I have had some terrifying dreams that were full of strange, sinister people, doing bizarre things. In these dreams I was aware of a fearsome sense of evil.

Once while addressing a group, I recalled such a dream. One woman in the audience suggested that perhaps I was "demon-possessed" since I had had several such dreams in a row. I answered her with several facts that should be remembered by all Christians, especially those who are entering a contemplative life.

First, no one can be God-possessed *and* Satan-possessed. Christians are filled with the Holy Spirit when they are baptized, and the Holy Spirit would certainly not countenance any "demons" living in the same place. The enemy may harass us, but having once been born again, we are sealed as Christ's own *forever*.

Second, it was obvious that this woman had never encountered a person who was *really* possessed by anything evil; if she had, she couldn't then have made such a suggestion. Christians are able to discern the presence of raw evil in their midst, should such a person be near; but they rarely see anyone really given all the way over to Christ's enemy. Most people are still alive in the battle.

Third, the recent surge of "deliverances" of demon-possessed or demon-obsessed Christians is not scriptural at the least and may be blasphemy at the most. Jesus mentioned the unforgivable sin for the first time to those who suggested that he had his power from Beelzebub. We should be far more careful of those who are indwelt by God's Spirit than to suggest that they may be occupied by another—an evil—force. Miriam was given a temporary case of leprosy as punishment for criticizing Moses, the "Lord's anointed". Who are today's anointed if not those who are born again in Christ?

Fourth, the evil we encounter in our dreams is very likely the dark and unpleasant side of our collective human nature. Psychologists who follow Dr. Carl Jung sometimes refer to certain modes of thought (both evil and good) as "archetypes," because they seem to occur in many people. They believe these archetypes are important aspects of being human. Some people believe that the most evil archetypes of all are what the theologians call original sin. Therefore, just as the comic-strip character Pogo suggested, "We have met the enemy, and he is us!"

Last is a fact that we all know too well: Where spiritual growth abounds, there the assaults of the world, the flesh, and the devil abound also. Just as we start to make some headway in prayer, we will next face temptation. This is part of our training and part of the silly plot by Satan to discredit his one enemy, Jesus Christ.

We need not fear this assault; we need only to be sensitive to its onset. The enemy is *like* a roaring lion; he is not a roaring lion. "Stand up to the devil," said James, "and he will turn and run from you."

The "heavenly" dream comes all too seldom. A woman in a retreat group once told us of a dream that made nearly everyone present sigh with envy:

> I found myself in a beautiful place of deep, shimmering blue, and I realized that it was the source place of all the music in the universe. I was seated at a loom, and trying to weave; but my work was in vain. Finally, I realized that I had only to put my hands up on the warp, and then bring them down, to make a beautiful pattern appear. As this richly colored weaving came, so came the music. I was weaving immortal, infinite music.

This dream was, indeed, a gift of gold and frankincense! Fortunately, the woman had recorded her dream and so was able to recall it. The more we write or tell, the more we will remember.

As we persevere in prayer, so we grow as dreamers. The

"left hand" becomes more "dexterous." And the more we dream, the easier it is to pray. God "breaks through" in as many areas of our life as we will allow and as quickly as we can stand it.

Even ancient peoples have known that dreams are related to the spiritual world around them; some tribes have even used drugs or herbs, believing that these hallucinogens would bring them closer to that world. Christian meditators need not go to such lengths. The One we call God does not offer a stone instead of bread; if we ask the One who guards our sleep for the gift of spiritual dreams, God is glad to answer.

In Scripture there are hundreds of examples of God's people giving dreams a holy importance. The dream of the ladder came to Jacob at a time when he might have had nightmares of anxiety instead. He and his mother had tricked his father into giving his blessing to Jacob, and Esau was in a dangerous mood. Jacob, heading for his family homeland, was shown a sight that saints would have given their lives to see. Already, God was showing Jacob that he had been chosen, set apart, and made holy enough to father the twelve tribes. Years later, near this same border, Jacob "wrestled all night" with some-one who changed Jacob's name to Israel. This "wrestling" may have been a dream with great spiritual import. The prophets were, of course, full of dreams that could help determine the fate of the nation. Near the end of Matthew's Gospel, we are told that Pilate's wife sent her husband a message saying, "Have nothing to do with that righteous man, for I have suffered much over him today in a dream" (Matthew 27:19).

One common fallacy is that dreams cannot be the stuff of heavenly gifts because they are the result of "primitive think-ing." Another fallacy is that such dreaming does *not* belong to people of the Reformation tradition.

These assumptions, however, are incorrect. Many early church fathers who are still respected as learned doctors of the faith—including Clement, Justin Martyr, and Tertullian—

spoke of dreams as important events. In fact in the third century, Tertullian wrote a lucid and discerning book, *The Anima*, which examines the nature of the individual soul. In his book he wrote about what modern scientists call REM (rapid-eye-movement) sleep. And it was Tertullian who wrote, "Is it not known to all the people that the dream is the most usual way that God reveals himself to man?"[2]

Later, Constantine the Great dreamed the explanation of his vision of the Chi-Rho. He had the vision of the Greek letters and then saw the message, "In this sign, conquer." But the vision was mysterious to him until he dreamed of Christ carrying the sign in his hand. It was this dream that converted Constantine to Christ and spared the lives of thousands of Christians who would have been martyred by the heretofore pagan government.

So when did dreaming fall out of spiritual fashion? It was probably around the time of the medieval scholar Thomas Aquinas, who in the thirteenth century promoted Aristotle's system of ideas through Christian Scholasticism.

This school of thought maintains that we can know God only through our reason and through literal perception by our five senses and that anything inexplicable is to be ignored. The death of the dream did not come at the hands of the reformers but at the hands of a medieval monk!

In fairness it should be noted that after many years of writing and study to prove his points, Aquinas had a mystical experience. We do not know what he experienced; we only know that he called everything he had previously done or written, "Mere straw."

Now people are beginning to take their dreams seriously again. Catherine Marshall, in her book *Something More*, devoted a good deal of time relating her dreams and suggested that her dreams changed as her relationship with Christ changed. During her long illness she dreamed (after a series of anxiety dreams) of hearing the hymn "Blessed Assurance, Jesus Is Mine."

"God's message to me was plain and oh, so welcome," she wrote. This outstanding Christian writer received her dreams as mysterious gifts in the dark night of her sickness and went on to make them part of her ministry.[3]

Recently, I had a wonderful dream; in fact, it was almost awesome. In my dream I got a telephone call from the rector of my parish church, asking me to come to the Salvation Army center to assist at a special service. When I arrived at the center, I saw my pastor, standing to one side. A woman was playing a piano while people sang, danced, and marched. My pastor indicated a beautifully carved old pump organ, and I joined the music-making. A Salvation Army band was playing with us, and I recognized the hymn.

After we had played together for a while, I was asked to put on my church lay reader's vestments. Then I went through a tunnel of raised hands, something like playing the singing game "London Bridge," while the band and the piano played and we sang. The "tunnel" went on for at least a mile. When I emerged, I looked at the great throng of joyful, singing people.

"This is wonderful," I said. "But who *are* you people?"

They looked at me wonderingly and cried in a great voice, "Why, Kristen! We're the church triumphant!" And with that, we all began to sing again. I awoke, singing the third verse of "Onward, Christian Soldiers" aloud!

Like Catherine Marshall, I could see God's message clearly. I tend to be an overly sensitive self-doubter, but after this dream I vowed to quit questioning every aspect of my own ministry, whether it be writing a book or taking a pot of soup to someone who is sick. God's love letter of celebration, the Letter to the Hebrews, was meant, I believe, to remind us that God will direct our doings, as a royal priesthood of believers, if we will allow it.

Perhaps this *is* the latter day, when "young men shall see visions and old men dream dreams." Or perhaps God thinks we have had enough rationalism in the last eight centuries, and so God has sent camels over the deserts of our minds, bearing strange people who bring wonderful and exotic gifts. These strangers, these Gentiles, see God made manifest and tell it through the "left hand."

5

Brokenness and Rebirth

The sacrifice acceptable to God is a broken spirit;
a broken and contrite heart, O God, thou wilt not despise.
—Psalm 51:17

The prodigal son thought maybe he had it made, at last! Hungry for something better than husks in a pigpen, he began to devise a way to get back into his father's home. Walking along the road, he began to practice murmuring, "Father, I have sinned against you and against God. ... treat me as one of your hired servants." (Note that he did not say, "slaves." The prodigal son was a conniver *almost* to the end!)

But suddenly he encountered something unexpected: his father was *running* toward him! In their embrace, the son found himself tearfully murmuring, "Father, I have sinned against you and against God. . . ."

One of our Bible class members remarked, as we studied this parable, "I *know* he was really repentant, then. Love is almost impossible to resist."

Love, God's kind of love, is indeed almost impossible to resist. We do not really know whether the prodigal *began* his journey home sincerely aware of his own guilt, but it is almost certain that when he was faced with the power of his father's love, he was filled with true remorse.

As we seek God in the silence of contemplative prayer, we

soon begin to be filled with a very similar compunction. It comes as we struggle along the way, trying to work out our salvation. Perhaps we are simply trying to relieve our guilt feelings, maybe with no more real heart involvement than had the prodigal. Suddenly, we look up and see that God is *running* toward us, arms open, eyes filled with tears of joy.

We cannot resist God, and so we run, too, toward that embrace. As the Lord touches us, we are filled with an overwhelming, honest remorse for our own sinfulness.

There is a great difference between "compunction" and "feeling guilty." Guilt feelings can stem from many causes; they are psychological, not spiritual, phenomena. While guilt feelings may cripple us emotionally, the conviction of sin—actually *being* guilty—is always accompanied by the knowledge that God can and will forgive us, in the shed blood of Jesus Christ. And each time we are forgiven, we are renewed and regenerated.

Contained within the parable of the prodigal is the assurance that God's love is always waiting for us, even before we ask forgiveness. The father of the story was pacing up and down in front of the estate, watching and waiting. When he saw his son, there was no mention made of past hurts; one who was dead was alive, and celebration was in order.

At the time of conversion, we usually, in some way, confess that we are sinful by nature and ask to be regenerated; but this does not mean we can never sin again. If it did, Jesus would never have told us to include "forgive us our trespasses" in the Lord's Prayer.

An opinionated woman I know involved me in a discussion of conversion one day. As we went on, it became obvious that her idea of conversion was a one-time-only confession of sin. When I asked her how she handled her sins in the present, she said, "Well, I have found that I can now lead a completely sinless life." She did not mean that *God* saw her life as sinless because of her justification in Christ; she meant that she just plain never sinned any more!

This woman's problem stems from taking one Scripture and ignoring another. She had taken First John's "Little children, sin not" and ignored "Anyone who says he has not sinned is a liar" from the same Epistle.

Further, since she had always avoided the rather elementary (to her) sins of the flesh that she had been taught were wrong at the time of her girlhood conversion, she failed to grow in her understanding of the nature of sin. She had always eschewed drunkenness and smoking and adultery, but she had missed the fact that she was sharp-tongued, chronically angry, and sometimes even cruel.

The sad truths that her employees feared her, her husband was lonely and neglected, and her children were seriously maladjusted did not reach her as evidence of sin; in fact, she saw those things as "inferiorities" in others, and thus added pride to the list of sins of which she was unaware.

The saved, the converted, need to continue in the scrupulous mortification of the "natural person." This is a great part of what Dietrich Bonhoeffer called "the cost of discipleship." Further, our sense of sin becomes more scrupulous as our devotion to centering prayer grows.

Perhaps as mature Christians we aren't unbearably tempted by the sins of the flesh (usually identified as committing adultery and misusing alcohol) but we are probably still vulnerable to being uncharitable or harboring angry thoughts toward a rival. Most of us are capable of reacting with inner anger or self-pity no matter how spiritually advanced we become.

But as we allow our spirits to be broken, our flesh and personalities to be mortified, and our hearts to be emptied so that God may enter anew, we are becoming different people. No one is left unchanged by the exercise of confession and penance, nor by the experience of awe.

I am fond of saying. "Look, all God wants is *everything!*" And C. S. Lewis said it much better when he wrote:

Christ says, "Give me All. I don't want so much of your time and so much of your money and so much of your work: I want You. I have not come to torment your natural self, but to kill it. No half-measures are any good. I don't want to cut off a branch here and a branch there, I want to have the whole tree down. I don't want to drill the tooth or crown it, or stop it, but to have it out. Hand over the whole natural self, all the desires which you think innocent as well as the ones you think wicked—the whole outfit. I will give you a new self instead. In fact, I will give you Myself: my own will shall become yours." [1]

As we persevere in interior prayer, Christ is lovingly nudging us to confess and discontinue our sins. Unlike the woman in a preceding paragraph who thought she was sinless, we are aware that our tempers are sometimes short, our manners unloving, and our hearts swelling with pride—the devil's own sin. Christ is merciful enough to want to keep working, making us fit for the heaven toward which we are headed.

The atonement is complete: Jesus Christ on the cross was, and *is,* a full, perfect, and sufficient sacrifice for sin. But as we grow in the faith, we discover that our wedding garments are sometimes dirty or tattered and that we need to accept God's gracious offer of forgiveness yet one more time.

There are two "sisters" who walk with contemplative Christians: the confession of sin (including both our own shortcomings and the sins of the world) and the confession of awe. No sooner do we experience compunction for sin than we are awed by Christ's action in human lives.

One evening several years ago I boarded a 747 headed for Rome and points beyond. Seated a few rows behind me was an old Hasidic Jew, a man with a great white beard and the traditional black hat and suit. He carried a string shopping bag full of water and kosher foods, not trusting the airline to meet his dietary restrictions. I awoke very early in the morning as the big plane flew into the dawn over the French coast. I got up to look out and saw this same old man wearing his tasseled prayer shawl over his head and shoulders. He held his little prayer book as he stood near the window, bowing his head and murmuring, thanking the Lord God for another day. Tears of devotion were visible on his wrinkled cheeks.

A few weeks later, I stood before the western wall (or what

some call the Wailing Wall) in Jerusalem, gazing at the great stones and noting prayers written on paper and stuffed into the chinks of this last vestige of Herod's great temple. On my left was an older woman who dug her fingers into the stone, weeping. Her arm was tattooed with a number that told me that she had once been in a concentration camp.

Suddenly I was seized with horror as I thought of the Holocaust, of the many attempts to eliminate God's Chosen People, and of all human inhumanity to other humans. I could see that magnificently devout old man, who had undoubtedly endured being called "sheenie" or "kike" or even worse, greeting Yahweh's morning. I saw the woman weeping at the wall. In my imagination I saw bodies of children stacked after being gassed at Auschwitz. I thought of the men, women, and children whose lives had either been snuffed out or left without meaning by the World Wars, the Korean War, and the jungle war in Southeast Asia during the 1960s and early 1970s. And I saw, above all these and looking down upon them, the crucified Christ.

Later in that day I visited the garden tomb. As I sat in the empty grave, some of those overwhelming images passed. Although I didn't forget the incident, the fact of the resurrection was so present that I didn't continue to be paralyzed with grief, as I was for a while at the wall.

Three years later, in the Communion service that ended a meditation retreat, the minister asked that we silently pray for the sins of the world. All at once, that same great tableau of grief and cruelty presented itself to my mind. As I ate the bread and drank from the cup, tears were running down my cheeks. I was experiencing one of God's great gifts—the *right* to ask forgiveness for the sins and injustices of the whole world, and a feeling of awe for that forgiveness.

Christ's first charge to the new church, the charge to forgive sins, came on Easter night. The disciples huddled behind closed doors in fear and confusion. Suddenly, Jesus was there. He showed them his wounds, greeted them with peace, and breathed on them. Then he said, "Receive the Holy Spirit. If you forgive the sins of any, they are forgiven; if you retain the sins of any, they are retained" (John 20:19-23).

The crucifixion and the resurrection have given us the privilege to ask God's forgiveness for all humanity's own sinful nature. "If any one does sin, we have an advocate with the Father, Jesus Christ the righteous; and he is expiation for our sins, and not for ours only but also for the sins of the whole world," says 1 John 2:1-2.

When a person begins to use a centering prayer and spends time in meditation, he or she inevitably is brought to this moment of remorse. I am always intrigued by this because this deep regret for sin comes *before* I ever tell prayer groups about it. A group might have three or maybe four meetings; then one night, ten hands will go up when I ask if anyone has anything to share.

"I was doing my morning meditation, and I suddenly got a picture of all the hurt or hungry people in the world, with their hands outstretched to Christ," one student, who was an artist, said excitedly.

"I was saying my 'centering prayer' as I fell asleep, and I started to cry," said a shy, soft-voiced young woman. "I thought of all the sins God had forgiven in *me,* and then those that everyone else had been doing since the beginning of time, and it was unbearable. I prayed for Christ to return."

"I didn't see any pictures," said a no-nonsense banker whose life-style was radically changed by the use of centering prayer. "I just suddenly realized what Jesus suffered for on the cross. I wanted to ask God to let the whole world be free of sin, but I wasn't sure I should pray that way."

I told him he should pray whatever way the Holy Spirit was telling him to pray, since we do *not* tell anyone how to let God work in his or her individual life.

When this compunction and awe comes over people, I always tell them that if they really want to know what Jesus endured on the cross (besides agonizing death by crucifixion), they can read the curse in Deuteronomy 28. Moses told the children of Israel that if they broke the Judaic Law, this is what would come upon them. We know that they *did* break the Law, and we also know that Jesus Christ himself suffered the fullness of the curse. Perhaps the sweetest comment I ever heard in this department was from the old lady who broke down at a retreat and said, "Poor Jesus! When I think of my sins and everyone else's, I feel so sorry for that boy!"

Your experience may show you that with each overwhelming realization of the sin of the world comes a new recognition of God's role in human history. *To see sin is to see Christ come and offer himself for it.* And to pray for the forgiveness of sins is to have an overwhelming experience of awe. We visualize Jesus ministering. Or if we aren't visualizers, we *sense* the work of the atonement.

Where sin abounds, there grace abounds, and grace is always disproportionately great. It is because of this fact that we are awed! Soon this awe colors our world, and we begin to live in a transformed state much of the time. Our lives at this point are very likely taken up with worship, even while we study or eat or work or talk. We are aware of the magnificence of creation when we just look at one blade of grass or one autumn leaf.

Awe stems from the premise that God is other than us. Unlike those who adhere to the religions of Asia, we do not believe that we and God are made of the same stuff and that through proper meditation we will remember one-with-Godness. But for the Christian, meditation is the route to a broken spirit and a contrite heart. This spirit and this heart God has promised not to despise! Apparently Jesus never got angry at a sinner, but he was very clear with those who thought they were above sin.

When we confess sin, we are put before the throne of God in grace; as we continue to pray, we sense more and more our awe of God's majesty. It is this "otherness" that brings us to our knees in adoration as well as in sorrow for sin and in surrender to God's goodness.

They walk together, these two "sisters": penitence and awe. At each breath of prayer, we experience the one; and as we release that breath, we know the other. Meister Eckhart says, "The eye with which I see God is the eye through which he sees me. . . ."[2]

6

The Golden Calf

When the people saw that Moses delayed to come down from the mountain, the people gathered themselves together to Aaron, and said to him, "Up, make us gods, who shall go before us . . ." (Exodus 32:1).

Christians, even those who are spiritually very mature, are always subject to temptation. As we grow in our faith, we may find it easier to leave the "sins of the flesh" behind us; our temptations seem, now, to leap out of our very prayer life.

"Why was my father not healed when I prayed?" we may wonder.

"I hear about people praying for cars and money all the time. When do I get a miracle in my life?" we may wail, in imitation of the prodigal son's brother.

"I am in prayer all the time, yet nothing seems to be going the way it should," we may cry to God.

When worldly wants begin to supersede our adoration of God's perfect will, we are sometimes tempted to call upon the visible power of the "real world." We may grow impatient with God's timing, or we may bring preformed ideas to our prayer life and let our worship begin to stray.

This is what happened to the Israelites while they waited for Moses to come down from Mount Sinai with God's Word. These

Exodus Hebrews felt alone and insecure; they wanted the reality of a god they could see. They wanted guarantees that the
god could see and hear them and answer their prayers—just
as we sometimes do.

Like the Israelites, we may need to learn that we cannot
expect God to respond to our preconceived notions but rather
that we were made to respond to God.

Moses and the mountain were shrouded by a terrible cloud
of unknowing; for the contemplative Christian, the silence found
in the prayer of union with God may sometimes seem just as
occlusive and unreal. Furthermore, we may have, erroneously,
come to expect and claim God's answers to our needs. Even
though we don't consciously seek graven images to worship,
we do find other golden calves to occupy our minds when
God's response to us does not seem to be forthcoming. We
sometimes indulge our whims, using the world's tools—sym-
bolized by the gold of the Egyptians—to rationalize our claims
upon God.

There is always the possibility that the contemplative life will
sometimes seem slow and unsatisfactory (not the terrible
emptiness of the "dark night of the soul" but simply a period
of boredom or even mild rebellion). In this age of instant grat-
ification, we are tempted not only to think in terms of the hope
of glory but to live in expectation of it. We may even tend to
forget that we were bought with a price and that the price was
the blood of the Lord Jesus Christ.

When Moses came with Joshua into the camp and saw the
people committing idolatry, he cried out, "Who is on the LORD's
side?" Then he charged the faithful to slay those who would
not attest to their belief in the living God. Likewise, among the
first things that any pilgrim needs to do is mercilessly to cut
away any attitudes toward worship and prayer that he or she
has transferred from the world, in much the same way as the
Levites slaughtered those who worshiped the calf.

Where did the people get the gold to make the calf? You will
remember that when the Passover was completed, the Egyp-

tians gave earrings and other gold ornaments to the people of Israel, to speed them on their way. Now, in the desert, the people were trying to mix this gold from Egypt with the worship of the one, invisible Lord. (See Exodus 12:35-36, 32:3-4.)

When we come into new awareness of God though meditation, it is dangerous to try to apply the world's ideas, our Egyptian gold, to our relationship with God. God has told us, over and over, throughout Scripture, that we are not to be an adulterated product. Do not mix wool and linen, God tells us; do not yoke this animal and that one together, do not eat flesh and milk together; do not marry the daughters of Canaanites; and when you enter the Promised Land, look neither to the right nor the left, but stay on the narrow path. Therefore, we need to cut away our false and worldly notions about spiritual life, resisting the desire to rationalize them as excusable. It is not our job to condone what God would redeem.

Some of the most common bits of "Egyptian gold" are the infusions of common worldly values into the expectations we have from our own spirituality; they include the belief that we should worship God only as long as that worship benefits us.

Beware of the leaven of the technologists! By this, I mean the belief that we must watch for results when we pray. The world has given us a message that says that if we take this pill, our headache will go away instantly; if we employ this bit of psychology on the job, our superiors will immediately note our abilities; if we pour hot water onto this substance, we will have a twelve-pound roast or a party-sized pot of coffee in moments.

Our homes are full of this kind of magic. I have a microwave oven that bakes a potato in four minutes and a food processor that makes peanut butter faster than I can open a new jar. Perhaps our subconscious thought is that if modern technology can do all this for us, surely God can do more. Isn't this true?

God can and does do more, but God's kingdom is not of this world; if we start confusing kingdoms, looking for either central or peripheral benefits from meditation that God never promised, we are headed for disappointment.

How often have you heard someone say, "I tried church (or prayer or Bible study or meditation), but I don't get anything out of it"? This "anything out of it" usually means obvious physical, financial, or spiritual benefits. We seem to think that if we don't have instantaneous healing of any illnesses, sudden manifestation of material success, or a prayer experience comparable to the Revelation to John, our Christianity "isn't working."

To further poison the wells of our own spirituality, there is the popular belief that meditation should be part of a health program, to be used to lower the blood pressure or some other physical benefit, along with a low-cholesterol diet, jogging, and vitamins.

Here is the truth as I know it. Using a constant phrase of prayer, plus one or two daily periods of sitting quietly, may very likely give us slower heartbeats and lowered blood pressure. There is very likely a beneficially altered brainwave. But these results are not guaranteed, nor should they be the sole reason one seeks God.

"I am the Lord!" God cries from the holy mountain. If we can get the same benefits from meditation with God as we do from, say, physical exercise, will that satisfy the Lion of Judah?

We were made for God. "We are the people of his pasture, and the sheep of his hand," says Psalm 95:7. We must remember that we were made for God's pleasure, as the objects of God's love, and not the other way around. We did not create God so that we could feel good, get rich, or have a "golden calf" to believe in. Meditation, contemplation, the prayer of union, the breath prayer—these are ways to fulfill the commandment to "pray without ceasing," not ways to achieve health or riches or other valuables from the "real world."

"Lay not up for yourselves treasures upon earth, where moth and rust doth corrupt, and where thieves break through and steal," said Jesus. Instead, he said, "Lay up for yourselves treasures in heaven, where neither moth nor rust doth corrupt, and where thieves do not break through and steal" (Matthew 6:19-

20, KJV). Jesus finished these remarks by adding that where one's treasure is, there will the heart be also. The treasure we seek is the Giver, not the gifts. We seek the throne of God and must not be tempted to stop and bow before worldly thrones.

How, then, do we catch ourselves when we seem to be slipping out of the habit of contemplative prayer and meditation, when anything—a soccer game on television, a conversation, a new magazine—seems more attractive?

We must start by using the tools that God provides in Scripture; prayer, penance, praise and perseverance. First, in prayer, tell God how bored or restless you feel. Be absolutely honest; say, "I'm not miserable, Lord; I'm just bored and restless, and I seem to have lost the little 'breath prayer' that I had been saying." Go on with this as long as it takes to empty yourself. *Kenosis*, self-emptying so that we may be filled with God, is not an instant procedure; it is, rather, a lifetime process. Telling ourselves that we are emptied when we are really full of feelings of self is not enough.

Tell God how busy you've been, how much you have on your mind, and how disappointed you are in yourself and even in God. Go ahead! God never smote anyone for honesty, and this kind of prayer is the only way to the next step, which is to ask God to restore your prayer of the heart or to give you a new one.

After you have asked, then begin immediately to use either your old phrase of meditation or a new one; don't wait for some handwriting on the wall or for the "Spirit to move you." The Spirit of God has already moved you to pray; now, like Job, you must put on fine garments and use your "own right hand [to] give you victory" (Job 40:14).

Then do repent and do penance. Tell God you are sorry that you're so far from conforming to the Son's image, so lax about doing what God is asking you to do and be. Do an actual penance or "turning step"; perform some small act of worship and study, such as reading the five praise psalms (146 through 150). These psalms will put you in condition for the next step of total praise.

Praise God. Praise is not thanksgiving. We give thanks for what God does; we give praise for what God is. Praise God for God's divine nature and majesty, for everything you can think of that describes God in your mind's eye. Read those five psalms again, and find some others (such as Psalm 29), or read Isaiah 6, to visualize almighty God.

The last phase, the one that must last forever, is perseverance. "He who endures to the end, will be saved," said Jesus in Matthew 10:22; and, "if we endure, we shall also reign with him," wrote Paul to Timothy (2 Timothy 2:12). Note that God's message is not that we must be brave and alone, trying our human best; Paul uses the words "endures with him" to remind us that everything we experience our own "High Priest" has also known and endures with us.

Perhaps one of the most insidious of our spiritual games is "I tried that." "Pray, repent, praise," God tells us, and we say, "But I tried that." We give the same answer when God tells us to tithe or to get up early for study or worship or to make friends with the grouch who lives on the corner.

"I tried that!" we say, melting our gold over the desert fire. "And it didn't work" we add, and out comes this "golden calf" of self-defined spirituality rather than the kind of spirituality that takes us over the Jordan and into the Promised Land.

But if we listen very, very closely, we may hear God's voice calling from the holy mountain and saying, "Try again! The one who perseveres to the end will be saved."

7

The Lord's Prayer:
A Model for Meditation

> He was praying in a certain place, and when he ceased, one of his
> disciples said to him, "Lord, teach us to pray, as John taught his
> disciples." And he said to them, "When you pray . . ." (Luke 11:1-2).

The abbreviated version of the Lord's Prayer in the Gospel
According to Luke is preceded by an interesting scrap
of conversation. Even though the disciple had Jesus,
the Incarnation of God, he wanted to make sure he also had
everything that John the Baptist's disciples had!

We don't know how or what John taught his followers. We
do know, however, that Jesus was not inclined to deny His
disciples' spiritual requests. He sometimes scolded them for
their lack of faith; yet He always met their needs. He did not let
Thomas spend his life wondering whether there had been a
real resurrection. He did not let Peter drown when he sank into
the sea while trying to walk. And He did not ignore this disciple's request, "Lord, teach us to pray. . . ."

But the Lord's Prayer is more than just a way to pray; it is
the way to pray, the model on which every other address to
God might securely be constructed. Further, the Lord's Prayer
is, for many, the touchstone in meditation.

Consider its clauses and phrases (here used in the most
traditional language), and then let your own creativity run free,

stripped for action, letting Jesus teach you to pray, as he did in this prayer:

"OUR FATHER." When we think of God as Father, and let the meaning of that idea penetrate through the intellect into the emotional and spiritual levels of ourselves, we may, like Teresa of Avila, be unable to go further. She wrote that many times in beginning her daily office, she was seized by such a rapture at the thought of God as Father that she could not go on.

Say the words; close your eyes. Think about the fact that no matter what happens, we have a heavenly Father who loves us enough to send his only Son to die for us. Remember that before the world was made, God knew how each of us would be; God loves us exactly the way we are and is willing always to redeem that personality.

It doesn't matter whether we have, or had, good earthly fathers. God has implanted in us a vacuum, and at these words, "Our Father . . . ," the vacuum begins to fill.

No matter how beautiful or ugly we are, inside or out, or no matter how we succeed or fail on earth, God remains our heavenly Father and we continue to be God's children, made righteous by the sacrifice of Jesus.

Take a few moments to let the words "Our Father" vibrate and make their own joyous rhythm within you. Receive God's fatherhood with gladness, with exultation; and let this exultation manifest itself in silence and devotion.

"WHO ART IN HEAVEN." Heaven may sometimes seem too high for us to reach, too far away to stretch toward; yet Jesus has shown us that heaven is within us, among us, around us. The kingdom of heaven is as close as prayer, as intimately a part of us as our own breathing, as far away as hatred or despair or apathy.

Let the thought that heaven is within you supplant any other thoughts you have at the moment. In your spirit's eye, be in heaven and let heaven be in you. At the center, you can find the elders, throwing down their crowns in absolute adoration.

Watch them; throw your own crown down. Hear the angels crying, "Holy! Holy! Holy is the Lord!" and join them. Let the words "Holy, holy" repeat at the same rate as your heartbeat.

As this rhythm of holiness begins to shape your meditation, realize that within you is the heaven where everything else is an interruption to the adoration of God. Know that heaven is at the center of your being and yet occupies the entire universe. It includes all the galaxies and the great nebulae; it includes a baby being born and immense suns, which are also being born. Heaven, within us, among us, all around us, is God's answering gift to a broken and sorrowing world. Enter this heaven, and stay there, with an absolute, prayerful attention to God.

"HALLOWED BE THY NAME." Somewhere inside us and yet somewhere far beyond, transcending our lives, is the inner tabernacle, the holy place. In this central chamber of adoration, the name of God is constantly being sung, shouted, whispered, and intoned—spoken in creation, spoken in love.

Rest in God's names and let them be ". . . nigh unto thee, in thy mouth . . ." (Deuteronomy 30:14). Silently repeat the names of God, letting them rest soundlessly in your mouth.

How many names can you name? Yahweh, Adonai, the Lord; the Lord Almighty, the Lord Most High, Jehovah-jireh, El Shaddai . . . Jesus, Y'shua, Christ, Messiah, Agnus Dei, the Lamb of God; Emmanuel, God with Us; the Lion of Judah; the Son of man, the Son of God . . . the Holy Spirit, the Teacher, the Earnest for our Salvation, Giver of Life. . . .

Let them cascade down from the deepest recesses of the mind and spill onto the day. Remember that if God's name is holy, then so are those "'people who are called by my name'" (2 Chronicles 7:14). As Christians, haven't we taken one of God's names? Contemplate in awe the name of God.

We can find grace in this holy place of God's name. We can find it alone in our prayer and meditation, or we can find it corporately in the celebration of the Lord's Supper. We can experience grace with exultation as we did perhaps at the moment we first came to God, or we can experience it in deep silence in the holiest of holies.

We can become holy whenever we reach out and touch the tassels of God's garment; in this holiness our meditation leads us to silence. Contemplating the fact that God's name is hallowed, rest quietly in God.

"THY KINGDOM COME." Let the King return in your mind and say, "I was hungry. . . . I was naked. . . . I was in prison. . . ." Ask, "When did I see you hungry?" and let God answer. Let yourself be touched by one you fed, as well as by one you passed by or ignored. Was it Christ on the road today? How did you respond to him in disguise?

The kingdom life is first a life of worship, but it is also a life of service. He or she who would be great among us must learn to wash feet, to sweep a stable, to give a drink of water. Who knows? The feet might be Jesus' feet; the stable might contain the Babe in a manger; the drink might lead to a conversation about living water.

Sit upright, with hands held outward for God to fill your need. Realize that a kingdom life is one of giving and loving and sacrificing. When each of us on earth learns to love others more than self, to love the way Christ loved us and was ready to give his life, then God's kingdom will come.

In the day that we beat our swords into plowshares and give up coveting and competing and being spiteful, then the lion and the lamb will lie down together in peace. If we can let our own lives be redeemed by Christ, we can take the whole universe a little closer to redemption.

The kingdom life is action. It is a small or large favor done in love; it is the "Yes!" to God and the "Yes!" of love to one's neighbor or children or spouse or parents. God's kingdom comes, is born, when hearts are filled with love. Contemplate God's kingdom coming on earth, and think of yourself as a vessel for that coming.

"THY WILL BE DONE." Work your will in us, Lord; help us to be receptive to your gentle knocking at our hearts!

What is God's will for us? Do you remember? It is that we respond to God's yearning love. We do this in prayer as we behold God in heaven; we also respond to that love when we act it out by reaching out to someone who suffers.

God's will is always done by the angels. Clouds and clouds of them are dispatched to win God's wars, to take messages to barren women ninety years old, to say, "Hail, O favored one!" The angels cannot disobey; they have not even been tempted, so they do not know all the gospel. They are God's messengers and sometimes even God's message, these angels and archangels, cherubim, seraphim, these powers and principalities of heaven.

Yet God longs for more. That longing is to have *us* turn, see, and run to God. God has a deep longing for us to come willingly, wantingly, away from our own ways and let the perfect will be done in us. Though omnipotent and capable of forcing the divine will upon us, God waits, like a patient suitor, like Hosea, who waited for his wayward wife.

We need to know God in order to know God's will. We can know God in Scripture, in prayer, in dialogue with human beings, and in absolute attention to creation.

Hebrews 4:12 tells us that the Word of God is active and alive, cutting between soul and spirit, between joints and marrow, with the sharpness of a two-edged sword. Since the word here is *logos* (λόγος), it means more than "the Word" of the Bible. Logos is what came down and tabernacled with us for a little while, according to John 1:14. Jesus Christ is God's Word begotten in that first uttered Word before all worlds.

Close your eyes and see absolute darkness and hear complete silence. Then hear God utter that Word; and as this happens, see the first point of light, light that has nothing to do with the physical universe. As that point of light draws closer, see that in uttering that first Word, God the Son has, in his burgeoning love, poured out the whole plan of salvation.

The written Word, too, can be a source of delight to us. We need to pray that we will always be excited, that the written

Word will, truly, shear that cartilage between soul and spirit, so that we are not fettered but can think with the mind of Christ. We need to let the Word slice between joints and marrow so that no impediment, no crippled bone at the center of our understanding, can enter into our relationship with God. This is God's will: we are to take the Word, spoken and written, into ourselves with joy and exuberance.

"ON EARTH AS IT IS IN HEAVEN." In heaven there are no sick or hungry people nor anyone who is lonely or suicidal or addicted. We need to make this true on earth as it is true in God's realm—through action that springs from our love of God, from prayer, and from the depths of meditation.

There are undoubtedly no people who neglect their prayers in heaven. How could they? When we get to heaven, I believe that all we will want to do is kneel down and look at the face of God. So why not make that true on earth? Let us say to ourselves that we are already redeemed, already reborn. Let us acknowledge that, spiritually, we are already "in heaven" and heaven is in us. Eternity began for each of us at the moment our faith became active, when the Holy Spirit took up residence in us forever.

Now, contemplate bringing heaven into visibility; consider being a sign of heaven to a broken world. Let silence surround you, and regard the difference between heaven and earth with sorrow and compunction.

"Whom shall I send," calls the voice of God from the great throne, "and who will go for us?"

God is surrounded by angels; yet God is not speaking to them. In the loud silence of the divine presence, answer, "'Here am I! Send me' to make earth like heaven."

"GIVE US THIS DAY OUR DAILY BREAD." Think of all the words in the Bible about bread. There is the Passover; then Christ our Passover is sacrificed for us. There is Manna; then Jesus is the Bread come down from heaven. There is the shewbread in the tabernacle, and Christ is forever on the altar as the one perfect and sufficient sacrifice. There is bread not made from stones, and Jesus, the living stone whose flesh is true spiritual food. There were a few loaves of bread broken and given to thousands; and there is the broken body of our Lord Jesus Christ, given for the multitudes.

Imagine a slice of bread, suspended in the air, its fragile crust cracked, its texture looking fresh and filling. Now imagine that a pair of hands, with wounds in them, break the bread and someone says, "Take; eat. . . ."

The life in Christ is a story of spiritual bread that has come down for the filling of human need. As God sent manna to those who were starving on the desert, so we can act out God's love by giving both food for the body and food for the spirit to those around us who need it.

We can remember, too, as those hands break that bread, not to be so busy making a living that we do not make a life in Christ. When we meet him, face to face, we realize that our hunger can be stayed only with spiritual food, our thirst only with living water.

"AND FORGIVE US OUR TRESPASSES, AS WE FORGIVE THOSE WHO TRESPASS AGAINST US." Is Jesus crazy, leaving us a prayer like this to say? We, who are by nature so unforgiving, so competitive, so grudge-holding, so self-righteous?

Yes, he knows. He knows we need to forgive and be forgiven quickly before guilt or grudge can work their mischief in our lives. Not only do we have to forgive the publican who is beating his breast (that isn't too hard for those of us who are lifelong Christians), but we also must forgive the pharisee, the self-righteous, the pompous, the sadistic, and the manipulative. We have to forgive our mothers and fathers and Hitler and Idi Amin and our fifth-grade teachers and Jim Jones in Guyana and those people who think they need no forgiveness.

Unless we can forgive all these, we can spend eternity in silence—not in the silence of God's presence but in the silence of hell, where the voice of God is only a choking memory, where the sound of angels' singing cannot penetrate the thick murk. Until we forgive everyone who has ever touched our lives (even only in the newspapers), we are headed straight for the pit, ourselves unforgiven.

Do not dwell on the nature of hell as motivation to be forgiving. Instead, race to the cross where your unforgiving nature is crucified with Christ, who suffered the curse of sin for us. Let your mind wander to the person you like least; it is said that dislike for a person gauges the amount of love you have for God.

There is an apocryphal story about Jesus that I love to tell. The scene is heaven, and the wedding supper is laid at last. The bride, that is, Christ's church, is dressed and ready, redeemed, waiting. The saints and apostles wait. And yet Jesus lingers, looking out a window.

Finally, one of his disciples approaches him. "Master? The wedding is prepared; will you come?"

Jesus turns and regards his friend, pain showing in his eyes. "I was watching for Judas," he explains.

"AND LEAD US NOT INTO TEMPTATION, BUT DELIVER US FROM EVIL." We cannot even imagine God "tempting" us; the Letter of James reminds us that God never tempts. Never. What, then, are we asking? Those of us who resist using modern language in the Lord's Prayer might stop to think that in the language of the King James Version, we are asking God not to do something that God won't do.

However, we don't have to pray "right" in order to make God hear us; God waits like a nervous lover on our every word and always knows what we mean. In this request we mean, don't put us to hard testing, don't desert us in the time of trial, don't *leave* us in temptation.

Scripture says—in Deuteronomy 31:6, Joshua 1:5, and Hebrews 13:5—that God will never leave us or forsake us. Actually, there are five negatives in the Hebrew, "I will not,/ will not leave you,/ I will never,/ no, never,/ no never forsake you."

As you contemplate that idea—perhaps with a picture of Christ always at your side, defending, loving, and nudging—

let the tune to the old hymn "How Firm a Foundation" run through the music system of your mind; and hear the last verse say, "The soul that on Jesus hath leaned for repose, I will not, I will not desert to his foes; That soul, though all hell should endeavor to shake, I'll never, no, never, no, never forsake" (written in 1787 by John Rippon).

Meditate on what being delivered from evil really means. Remember that it means that since by a man came death, by a Man also comes the resurrection . . . and grace . . . the atonement . . . and being delivered from the enemy.

"FOR THINE IS THE KINGDOM, AND THE POWER, AND THE GLORY, FOREVER AND EVER; AMEN!"

As you think through this doxology, praising God for the kingdom and the power and the glory, let your word of prayer be "Amen, amen"; for the word means "Truly, truly."

8

Aslan's Country

"Inward and upward," Peter shouted.[1]

It was Aslan's country, all right. The children knew it. As they entered, they felt a steady pull from Aslan, who was leaping before them. "Inward and upward," they kept shouting; no matter how deep in the country they were or how high the mountains they climbed with Aslan, they wanted to go deeper, higher. They wanted more.

Aslan is, of course, C. S. Lewis's beautiful lion; he symbolizes Christ in stories that Lewis wrote for children. In the final book—*The Last Battle*—Aslan ends his world. After a final judgment, the children go to his country, and like most people who even *glimpse* Christ, they can't get enough of him or his country.

In the same way, most serious students of prayer discover that after a while they feel a little frustrated in their meditation and study. Their hearts are crying, "inward and upward!" They want *more*.

This is the time to extend boundaries in the Promised Land. If you have been using your prayer for centering during, say, two five- to ten-minute periods of sitting and praying, increase them by five minutes. I usually suggest that students add five minutes every week or month, depending on one's own temperament and inclination. I also suggest that twenty-five or thirty minutes, twice daily, is a good *maximum* amount for most uncloistered people.

There is, for some of us, a temptation to stay in the meditative field long after our timers have rung. This is the time to recall the discipline of stopping! But it does mean that it may be time to *deepen* the prayer time.

Teresa of Avila described the several stages of prayer as "four ways of watering."[2] She likened our prayer life to a garden in which God is the planter and we the waterers. To leave one kind of prayer for another does not mean that we have graduated from something elementary. We tend to grow in spiritual cycles and to complete all the stages of prayer before starting the cycle again.

The first method of "watering," according to Teresa, is mental prayer; "bringing a bucket of water from a well." Even this kind of prayer is beyond everyday petition; it is the first step in conscious adoration. Here we use our "centering prayer" or meditation in words. Here, too, belong the joys of Scripture meditation, which are described later in this chapter.

The second stage of prayer, that of recollection and quiet, Teresa calls "using a waterwheel turned by hand." Note that we are still, at this phase, making an effort; the waterwheel must be turned, although we are beginning to lose compulsiveness.

Our words of meditation may stop. Images are not brushed away completely but are more given over to God's imagery as we wait quietly upon the Lord, knowing the fullness of God's love and presence. Within this kind of prayer, we may re-collect ourselves and recollect the goodness of God. It is here that many are often brought to compunction, experiencing either in thought or in image the severe mercy of Jesus; others believe that here they receive guidance and direction.

The third stage of prayer, that of the "sleep of faculties," is likened to directing a stream along an irrigation ditch. The sleep of faculties is simply that moment when our ego-connections slip away; transfixed by the presence of Christ in the holy Trinity, we forget about self—physically, emotionally, and even spiritually—and allow God to operate within us.

This occurs when we trust God so deeply for our own salvation that we cease being preoccupied with our own lives at all and are content merely to be near God.

The last and best kind of watering, Teresa says, is that which we do not in any way control. It is the prayer of union, described as "rain from heaven."

In my Oregon yard, plants must be watered during our dry summer. Fortunately, we do not have to turn a waterwheel by hand; instead, we use a garden hose. But in the other three seasons, watering is free. It falls out of the sky onto our ground, creating the greenest grass, surely, in the whole world.

The water falling onto the earth becomes part of the earth itself, standing in pools until it drains into the soil. So it is with the prayer of union. We are joined in mystical oneness with God, nourished by God's "watering." God's holiness becomes our holiness, God's mercy our mercy, and God's love our love. There are no words in this kind of prayer, no thoughts or images; the senses are no longer asleep but transformed, made, even for a moment, like Christ's. This was Christ's desire that he expressed in his high priestly prayer on the night of his betrayal;

> "The glory which thou has given me I have given to them, that they may be one even as we are one, I in them and thou in me, that they may become perfectly one, so that the world may know that thou hast sent me and hast loved them even as thou hast loved me" (John 17:22-23).

Our first experience with this kind of prayer may be a little staggering. It is not that we are "out of control" or in a "trance"; people who meditate are always completely alert and able to respond to what is around them *if they choose.*

The mind-boggling part comes with our awareness of God's majesty and power, our sense of "things that cannot be told, which man may not utter" (2 Corinthians 12:4), to recall Paul once more. This apostle was so overwhelmed by the presence of God that he could not say whether he had his experience of heaven in his body or out of it. His senses were not asleep; he let himself be completely filled with Christ.

Once a young minister of another denomination visited one of my classes. He was obviously annoyed by what I was saying, and during the first opportunity for discussion, he suggested that my material was foolishness.

"I want to be part of the real world," he said gruffly. "There are people out there with real needs."

I asked him if he had a deeply satisfying prayer life and whether he believed his prayers were being answered. He hedged a little, and I said gently, "You came here to this class for something. I don't think it was to heckle me. I think you may be torn between what you think of as your calling, and what Christ is whispering to you."

He was silent for a few moments; but he didn't look offended. Finally he said that he would try what I was teaching for a few days "as long as it doesn't interfere with my real ministry." His "few days" started about three years ago, and to my knowledge, he is still brimming over with ministry because he is able to love Christ in his daily meditation and prayer life.

No one is underqualified for a job in Aslan's country, nor is anyone asked to do something he or she cannot. "Reality," as the world defines it, is diametrically opposed to what heaven believes. The young pastor in the previous story found that he was better equipped for the world around him and for the needs of "real people" when he was filled by the presence of Christ through centering prayer.

This time, when we desire more from prayer, is an excellent opportunity to investigate the rich possibilities in Scripture meditation. This kind of meditation almost always leads us from the "bucket" stage to the water wheel. The Word of God never goes dry nor does it lose its meaning to us when we are seeking more depth or when we are troubled or spiritually "on the desert."

Begin by choosing some recorded biblical events in the life of Jesus. Read the Scripture over several times until it begins to form a picture in your mind. Is Jesus riding into Jerusalem? See yourself somewhere in the throng. Let him speak to you or wave. Throw your cloak or a palm branch down for him. Look around at the others in the crowd.

Is Jesus speaking to the multitudes on a mountain? Choose a spot of grass or a rock to sit on. Listen to his words; allow yourself every possible physical sensation—touch the grass, listen to the sounds of birds in the date orchards, give the people in the crowd faces and names. Listen to the pitch and timbre of his voice. Look at his hands. Always let the words that Jesus is speaking be for you and then the Word of God will be "nigh you, even in your mouth." Let your spirit consume these words like food; Jesus is, after all, the "Bread Come Down." Permit your senses to respond to your spiritual needs, and make this moment in history a part of your soul's today.

Choose the major events in the life of Christ for these exercises. Experience the Nativity, the confounding of the scholars in the temple, the miracle of water turned to wine, the ministry, the betrayal. You need not be a *major* character in this play; you may not choose to be Peter but rather just an onlooker at the fireside in front of Caiphas's house on the Thursday of betrayal. Or you may stand beside John at the foot of the cross, wondering what will happen next, with the Master there dying.

Of course, Scripture meditation is not meant just for times of deeper seeking or meditative dryness. Whole retreats are planned around such exercises. Through them you can find a deepening understanding of Christ's ministry. Soon you may want to take other Scriptures, imaging the creation of the world, the parting of the Red Sea, the confrontation of Elijah by the priests of Ba'al. You may want to walk with Nehemiah around the walls of Jerusalem or watch Ezekiel's chariot of fire touch the earth. Whatever you select, be sure to:

- Pray before reading, for the inspiration of the Spirit.
- Select a passage for the day and note it in your journal. Read it carefully at least three times.

- After reading, imagine the scene and place yourself in it. Let the meditation "take its own shape."
- Stop when your timer rings.
- Record a few words in your journal about the experience.
- Thank God for the holy Word and say the Lord's Prayer.

The desire for new vistas of prayer or for a deeper relationship with Christ *may* manifest itself in a fervent desire for more prayer and fasting and study; however, it may soon become just the opposite—an inability to concentrate on meditation or even a dislike for prayer!

Medieval churchman John of the Cross called this restlessness the "dark night of the soul." Some Christians in the midst of such an experience may believe that they are found unworthy or that God's presence has been withdrawn from them. God is faithful! God *never* withdraws love and support from us and longs to pull us inward and upward until, like the bee that threw itself into the flower, we hurl ourselves with abandon into God's heart.

Sometimes people even give up their quest for the holy of holies at this point of dryness in prayer. "See?" they cry, pointing at their own empty hearts, "it was useless."

These persons have forgotten how lovers play "tag" together, "hiding" where they will surely be found by the other. "Catch me!" is not a rejection but an invitation! Thus we who long to be faithful know that we must *pursue* the Lord, just as the children pursued the sight of the leaping, golden-maned Aslan.

"After all," the people in those delightful books agree, "He's not a *tame* Lion!"

And God is not a tame God to be kept in a cage at the zoo and petted when we feel like visiting. God will not be kept shut up in a box or a cage or even in a vast solar system. This is the living God, whose hands might seem fearsome to fall into, who creates galaxies and suns and universes, and who is concerned over the tiniest atom of each DNA molecule in every human being. And we must be ready to follow, to chase if necessary, wherever God goes.

If we give up inner prayer because it has become difficult or because we suddenly find that it is no longer "rewarding," then we have stopped right at the point from which God would take us deeper into divine country. This is the time for faithfulness in prayer and devotion to reading Scripture. It is also a time for us to be quiet within, listening with renewed attention for the footstep of Christ.

If the exercises of disciplined prayer time and Scripture meditation are pursued with faithfulness even during a "dry" time, that period of spiritual growth may become a very rich one. And when the dark night is over, when we have responded to what seems like an empty universe by being quietly faithful to God's Word, our reunion with God's presence will be more beautiful than anything else we can imagine. Until then, the trick is to be faithful, *without* falling into Job's sin.

"What?" I hear a voice saying. "But Job did not sin!" But if he did not, then why did he repent in the forty-second chapter of that book? For many years I puzzled over this repentance of Job. What had he done, I wondered, to have to repent in dust and ashes? No matter how many times I read this ancient book, I could not find any sin in him.

Then one day, I was trying to write a fiction piece about a young woman who had seemingly lost her faith by falling into boredom and listlessness. I stopped at this point to look up the dictionary spelling for this particular deadly sin, checking to see whether the preferred spelling was "acedia" or the old Anglo-Saxon "accidie".

To my surprise, neither was listed! I looked in my *Handbook of Theological Terms,* by Van Harvey. It went from "absolute" to "accident" without a qualm. I called my pastor, who looked in his small, abridged *Oxford Dictionary.* Not there, either. Was this gloomy boredom, sometimes badly translated as "sloth," no longer a sin? Was Dante wrong in describing the fifth circle of hell, where sinners lay in black mire with dull smoke rising lazily around them?

But I know too well that acedia exists. (I later discovered that the *Oxford Unabridged Dictionary* acknowledged the presence of such a sin on earth.) I was forced by grace to think of a time in my own life when, physically ill and having problems in my professional life, I fell into a sadness, a fatal boredom. While friends urged me to rest and take it easy, Christ was nudging me to live, to affirm the power of his resurrection in my own life. Only when I confessed the sin of acedia to Christ did I begin to get well, physically and spiritually.

"Gird up your loins like a man," spoke God out of the whirlwind to Job. For too long Job had simply sat there being a victim, yet saying that he knew all about God. He affirmed that God was indeed God and could do what God wanted, giving and taking away. But never did he even *speak* to God until the Almighty addressed him.

"But now my eye sees thee; and therefore I despise myself, and repent in dust and ashes," he cried in Job 42:5-6. Immediately God told the three comforters to ask Job, now made righteous again, to pray for them; and God accepted Job's prayer. It becomes clear that we will not be righteous in Aslan's country if we prefer to believe that we are victims, abandoned by God.

After my prayer of confession and my acceptance of God's forgiveness, I entered a new depth of meditation. Once I spoke volumes of words to God; now I could only adore. Once I petitioned God constantly, both for my own needs and as intercessor; now, I would simply draw others into the circle of God's love, entrusting them to God's care.

My own centering prayer would stop almost immediately, but certainly not because of "dryness." I would sit for a moment or two, murmuring in my mind; then suddenly I would be lifted into a new kind of creation, where the presence of Christ in the Trinity was so awesome that words seemed superfluous. I began to understand, certainly on a smaller scale, what Paul meant when he said, "and heard things that cannot be told, that man cannot utter"(2 Corinthians 12:4) and what Isaiah experienced when he saw the Lord, with the train filling the temple, and heard the angels and archangels crying, "Holy! Holy! Holy!" (Isaiah 6:1-13).

Whatever we experience or think or believe in our prayer of the heart, we must remember that every picture of Jesus must contain not only the triumph of transfiguration or resurrection but also the sorrow of the Cross. Being centered in Christ does not mean freedom from pain or poverty; coming through the restlessness of the dark night does not guarantee us a per-petual morning in the soul. We are not promised a carefree life. What, in fact, *is* guaranteed is that we will die, daily, if we truly respond to him.

Dietrich Bonhoeffer said,

> The passion of Christ is the victory of divine love over the powers of evil. . . . Once again, Jesus calls those who would follow him to share his passion. How can we convince the world by our preaching of the passion when we shrink from that pas-sion in our own lives? On the cross, Jesus fulfilled the law he himself established and thus graciously keeps his disciples in the fellowship of his suffering. The cross is the only power in the world which proves that suffering love can avenge and van-quish evil. But it was just this participation in the cross which the disciples were granted when Jesus called them to him. They are called blessed because of their visible participation in his cross.[3]

The cost notwithstanding, all we need is a glimpse to want to know all of God! God will place us, like Moses, in the cleft of a rock, to see the back of God passing by—and we will forever long to see God's face. Even death will seem different after such a glimpse, for in death we are finally granted our heart's desire to see God face to face.

9

From the Tabernacle

For throughout all their journeys the cloud of the LORD was upon the tabernacle by day, and fire was in it by night, in the sight of all the house of Israel (Exodus 40:38).

Note: Use of this material may be harmful to your ego.

Most Christian books, especially the how-to-do-it kind, seem to contain a chapter full of "testimony." I have read books that told how people gained financial solvency, restored their marriages, and achieved much worldly success through some new style of prayer or tithing or Christian behavior. But there is a different, more important kind of "testimony."

Now, it came to pass that when the tabernacle was made according to the plan given to Moses, God showed acceptance by filling it with glory. The people *saw* something. The light of God's testimony, or Shekinah, was *visible*.

Throughout the history of worship in Judaism and Christianity, God has used *physical* evidences of divine action on earth and in heaven. God set a rainbow in the clouds as a visible sign of the covenant with Noah, and God asked of Abraham that males be circumcised, again as a visible covenant sign. Later, the evidence of God's direction and guidance was written on two stones, the tablets of the Law. The Israelites were afraid to proceed without that which they had *seen* in the pillar of cloud and the pillar of fire.

After the incident of the golden calf, Moses had to intercede with God, saying, "We can't make it without you, Lord, no matter how many angels you send along"(Exodus 33:12-17, author's paraphrase). The *visible* evidence of God's direction, the tablets of the Law, were also called the "tablets of testimony." Now, in the Old Testament "testimony" is also a translation of *shekinah,* which was the light of the glory of God that filled the tabernacle.

The tabernacle, its design and hangings and furniture, have often been compared to the inner person. There were places in the outer court where sacrifice was made for sin; the laver for cleansing was placed between the altar and the "tent of the testimony." Many other symbols in the making of the tabernacle are easily translated into aspects of the holiest part of the human soul.

There was no natural light in the holy place; the lampstand was the only source of illumination. Therefore, when we come into our own holy place in prayer, it is important that we do not bring with us "natural" light. Natural light, like the "natural man" (or woman) of Scripture, is not fit for the holy place. It is *natural* to lose one's temper and kill an enemy; God's "lampstand" of wisdom, found in the depth of prayer, heals what is natural. We are inclined to long for the "natural," meaning "innocence," forgetting that we are a fallen race and that the whole universe is in travail until Christ comes to redeem it.

Furthermore, since no light from the outside world was allowed in the holy place, this is also neither the time nor the place for psychological sophistry or pedantics.

God said to Moses, in Exodus 40:9, "You shall take the anointing oil, and anoint the tabernacle and all that is in it, and consecrate it and all its furniture; and it shall become holy."

In Exodus 19:22 and several other places, warning is given about the power of God. Those who are called to be part of the worshiping community are warned to be properly anointed "lest *[the LORD] break out against them"* (author's emphasis). The power of God was not a matter to be treated lightly, even by the chosen priesthood. To this day, priests in liturgical churches wear a ropelike cincture or girdle as a reminder that the Aaronic high priest had to wear such a rope so that he could be dragged out of the holy of holies if his sacrifice was not acceptable and he was killed by God.

In the same way, the interior prayer life of men and women is meant to be purified, holy, and consecrated to God. Otherwise, we may find ourselves playing with fire but not knowing what to do with it. William McNamara, a monk in Nova Scotia whose books bear reading, has said that some Christians get close enough to the fires of God to keep cozy and warm but not close enough to be burnt, consumed; only when we are led into and totally consumed by that fire, by that passion for Christ, are we fit for the company of angels and archangels![1]

We often speak of inspired preaching or teaching as being "anointed"—that is, as having God's holiness and creativity. But how do we anoint our own spiritual lives? This can only be achieved when we ask for consecration by the *Holy* Spirit, who is the "holying" Spirit as well as *being* holy.

And the evidence, the testimony? The Holy Spirit, according to theologians, exists to glorify the Son, even though the Spirit is, as the third person of the Trinity, a person to be worshiped and glorified. When the Holy Spirit is working though us and in us, Christ will be glorified in every moment of our lives.

The light of God's work does not hide itself under a bushel! It is always interesting to observe one whose life is a territory occupied by the Holy Spirit and shows forth the glory of Jesus Christ. I remember one man who came into a beginning group for centering prayer; the group hated him on sight. He said, "Praise the Lord!" until it sounded like a broken record. He was constantly getting messages from God for everyone, delivering them with the statement "The Lord told me to tell you. . . ." He listened very closely to every word I said as group facilitator, making sure I in no way contradicted his pastor's interpretation of the Bible. When I was sick in bed, he called to suggest that I had not claimed my healing or that my faith was thin.

And then the man began to meditate in earnest. (You know how it goes; given a cubit, God will take over the whole country!) He became quieter, more receptive, and much less sure of himself as the star of every show. He quit talking about "the work the Lord is doing" in him, and let the Lord actually *do* the work. Heretofore, he had always reported many symbols or images that he saw in his meditation, apparently believing that the holier one got, the more one "saw." Soon he learned that he was closer to God when he brushed images away.

Finally, that man began to grow in a *very* perceptible way. He is now gentle, merciful, and giving. He no longer rushes about helping people in an ostentatious way but offers his expertise and assistance humbly. The more he quieted himself through the centering prayer, the more we all were able to see Christ. The Shekinah glory of God was a testimony that could come only to a place consecrated, anointed, made holy by silent adoration, with the superfluous decoration of his human ego transformed into the "furniture" of the tabernacle.

Thus we get some basic ideas about the "testimony" or visible sign of God's presence as we grow in centering prayer. But at the other end of the Bible, in John's Revelation, we hear,

> ... a loud voice in heaven, saying, "Now the salvation and the power and the kingdom of our God and the authority of his Christ have come, for the accuser of our brethren has been thrown down, who accuses them day and night before our God. And they have conquered him by the blood of the Lamb and *by the word of their testimony* ..." (Revelation 12:10-11, author's emphasis).

For many years I assumed that the "word of their testimony" meant something like standing up at a midweek service and reciting the story of one's salvation, or perhaps talking about one's successes in using missionary zeal. Later I began to study very elementary New Testament Greek and was astonished to find that in this Revelation passage, the word "martyrias" ($\mu\alpha\rho\tau\upsilon\rho\iota\alpha$) is what we have translated as "testimony." This same Greek word is translated as "witnesses" in Hebrews 12:1 and as both "witness" and "testimony" in 1 John 5:7-11 and elsewhere.

It is fairly obvious that our word "martyr" is from the same root, and I began asking myself, What kind of witness, what kind of testimony will be demanded from me in order to have the Shekinah kind of testimony in the tabernacle of my own spirit? Is it perhaps true that the only real witness is the blood of the martyrs?

Several years after this puzzle began to work within me, I discovered that members of certain Jewish sects would not walk on that ground of the temple mount (Mount Moriah) in Jerusalem. It was their belief that the lost ark of the covenant was buried somewhere in the mount, and they did not want to place themselves between the ark and heaven.

It would be too easy, and perhaps verging on the arrogant, to dismiss this as only ignorance or superstition. In our written record of Yahweh's dealings are some rather spectacular examples of God's Spirit "breaking through." David's soldier was *killed* for touching the ark, although all he did was to keep it from falling; but he was doing someone else's job and was not purified.

The power of God is often likened to electricity, which can both light a city and destroy life. Holy things are for holy people, and to come close to the action of the living God may be dangerous to human life, as the passage from C. S. Lewis quoted in a previous chapter has reminded us. To be holy is to contain the Shekinah glory of God, to proclaim the word of our testimony; witness may be martyrdom. We have to give up our lives, either spiritually or physically or both, dying daily, to keep from putting unsanctified hands on the ark or to keep from placing our humanity between our spiritual lives and heaven.

Here, then, is one of those paradoxes God seems so un-
commonly fond of injecting into our lives. We are told that we
are to have life abundantly while dying daily. He invites us into
the holy place and yet threatens our lives if we enter. What can
all this mean?

As a Christian laywoman, it is not my job to write a compre-
hensive and profound text on theology; but I *can* give the record of my own devotional life. The paradox? It means that as
I grow in the Lord, I will have to die to the world—and in ways
I may not have yet dreamed. So far my blood hasn't been shed
in martyrdom, but daily some aspect of my personality "dies"
as a result of rather major spiritual surgery. God wants to empty
me of myself so that I may be filled with light, with Shekinah.

"Would any of you, having a lamp, hide it under a basket?"
cried Jesus in his Sermon on the Mount. "Let your light so
shine before [people], that they may *see* your good works and
give glory to *your* Father *who is* in heaven" (Matthew 5:16,
author's emphasis).

That "light" is, of course, the same light—testimony, witness,
or *martyrias*—that we have been talking about. It is the glory
of God, shining out of the tent of testimony so that all the
people of the Exodus could see it. It is the witness of lives and
words in the great celebration of victory in the church. And it
is the martyrdom—perhaps asking us only to die daily within
but perhaps asking us, someday, to stand with those who risk
death for the sake of their faith.

I once knew a young woman whose "light" truly did shine
before everyone. She didn't chatter endlessly about the Lord,
but it was clear from her behavior and her well-chosen words
that she was living her life for Christ.

One day a friend said she reminded him of "a Christian
against the lions."

"You're not afraid of anybody!" he, a nominal Christian,
added. "Aren't you afraid you'll get hurt?"

Her laughter was like light scattered by a prism. "What can
anyone do to me?" she teased. "Kill me?" and she laughed

again. Once given a firm vision of life with God, she was hardly threatened by the thought of loss of this life. She was like Paul, who, after having been "lifted up to the highest heaven," didn't honestly care if he lived or died. (This, of course, is not like the apathy found in depression. Paul was not suicidal; he simply had a glimpse of something he longed for.)

I do not recommend that we become careless or begin driving dangerously or otherwise throwing ourselves off the pinnacle of the temple. The purpose of life is to live; if it were not, God would have ordained a different plan. But as we murmur the words of our centering prayer and in that process suddenly see the wonders of the transfiguration, of Isaiah's vision, of Samuel's calling from God, and of that first Easter morning, we see that the concerns of our lives in the world are becoming noticeably less important.

The goals we strive for—be they graduating from seminary and being ordained or becoming parents or retiring with an annuity or getting a CPA—are suddenly left behind. We are impressed, as we meditate, with the *immediacy* of Christ. He *is* the"here and now," as well as the "someday" and "always." In him are the alpha and omega. He holds the beginning and the end; therefore, they are not our concern. Furthermore, he ordained a day called "today," in which we live and move and have our being.

I recently talked with a person of means, who had great material possessions but who seemed to be so mature spiritually that he did not *need* anything he had.

"Meditation is a reducing diet!" he said, and I asked what he meant, since I didn't seem to be losing an ounce.

"Since I started centering prayer, I've become almost thin enough to go through a needle's eye," he answered, grinning.

Loss of compulsive attachment is only one of the particles of the light that shines out of the tabernacle. To be "free in Jesus" means to live as he did, unfettered by the world.

We live in a society that makes much of its quest for security. Now, there is nothing unchristian about buying some life insurance or carrying a mortgage to buy a home or paying into the Social Security system. But our priorities must be kept straight. The most secure man in the world is a man in prison; he need not worry about what to wear or eat or what to do with his time. All that is securely taken care of.

But equally secure is the bird outside my window—secure not because of the strength of the bough it is standing on but because of its wings! To be "free in Jesus is freedom indeed," the freedom to fly with our own wings, not leaning on the strength of worldly values or material possessions.

What we are aiming for, as we empty ourselves of self and fill ourselves with God, is *radical obedience* to Jesus Christ. Radical obedience means more than legalism or slavish devotion to duty and prayer and the Bible. It means acting like Jesus: it means *really* having mercy and love toward the unlovable, *really* praying for our enemies, *really* taking off our cloak along with our coat, and *really* taking no thought for the morrow. And it means that we must actually die to self so that the testimony can pour out through the hangings of our holy tabernacle.

If centering prayer brings radical obedience to Christ, can we change the world? Possibly. But the first and most important mandate for Christians to heed is that *we* not be changed *by* the world. Centering prayer helps us to be in the world, not of it. Our anointed energies flow from a holy place.

Radical obedience schooled in centering prayer can be a powerful force *if* God has given one a public ministry or called one to be a social activist. How we are called and how we interpret God's Word are highly individual. That's the whole story of grace and how it works in our lives—making what we already are into what we are called by God to be.

Protestant mystics in a world threatened by pollution and famine and nuclear holocaust have particular kinds of problems for their "right hands" to solve. But the "left hand," the dreamer, reaches for Christ and begins to control our response to the world around us. Radical obedience is ridiculous—to the worldly. Mysticism is foolish—to the wise. The threshold of prayer is where the wise and worldly are confounded, where the divine "I Am" is greater than what is or was or ever will be.

10

Coming Down from the Mountain

The LORD our God spoke to us at Horeb and said, 'You have stayed on this mountain long enough. . . . I have laid the land open before you; go in and occupy it . . .' (Deuteronomy 1:6-7, NEB).

There are some people in the world whom God has called to live apart from society in a contemplative life. John the Baptist lived this way until he was called into ministry as the "one crying in the wilderness."

We thank God for those who live in cloisters and pray constantly for the world. Without them, the world might be more terrible than it is now. These people, and all intercessors, are like Aaron and Hur, who held up the arms of Moses to make the battle with Amalek a victorious one.

The rest of us, though, are called out of the rarefied atmosphere of the mountaintop to occupy the rest of the world. Daily, we seek Christ in meditation; daily, he sends us into a fallen world to bind up the brokenhearted, to bring the Good News to the poor, to proclaim liberty to the captives. Each day of life can be a "year in the Lord's favor," in which we give garlands to mourners and splendid clothing to those with a heavy heart (Isaiah 61).

A phrase attributed to a philosopher and mathematician of the sixteenth century, Blaise Pascal, states that every human has a God-shaped vacuum inside. It is, in fact, this very emptiness that has brought us to our knees, thirsty for the sweetness of Christ's presence, yearning for more and more of him, listening constantly for the sound of his voice.

"As the hart panteth after the water brooks, . . ." so have we sought the mysterious heart of God, knowing that although our salvation is completed in the perfect sacrifice of Christ, we are not here to remain smug and safe in that knowledge.

But what of the rest of the world? What about those captives waiting to be set free? How do we take the fruits of our prayer life into the world filled with child abuse, pornography, wife-battering, angry political exchange, traffic accidents, and death from cancer? And how do we get from the mountaintop to the street without suffering from shock or without compartmentalizing our Christ-life?

The disparity of the two worlds, God's and humanity's, is only a limited picture from a human perspective of the incredible gulf that our Lord crossed when he became incarnate. For over fifteen hundred years, some parts of the church have recited the Nicene Creed and bent their knees at the words "and was incarnate by the Holy Spirit. . . ." An awesome thought indeed! The "Grand Miracle," as C. S. Lewis calls it, began when Christ stepped off the throne and became an unborn child in the womb of a Galilean peasant girl.

When we feel confused at leaving our meditation to go to work or prepare breakfast for a family or perhaps open our eyes to a drab hospital room, we are experiencing only mild shock. Imagine the awe in heaven when God became flesh!

That God understands our confusions. Ours is not, the writer of Hebrews tells us, a high priest who can't sympathize with our weaknesses. Jesus is one who as a human being was tried in every possible way and found faultless. Because of this we can go boldly before the throne for mercy and help (Hebrews 4:14-16).

Most of us have gone to a retreat or church camp or prayer mission, often literally on a "mountaintop" at some resort or woodsy setting. We have come home, excited and inspired, only to discover that the retreat soon seems far away and the inspired teaching begins to look impracticable or unrealistic.

This experience can give us insight into the value of *daily* meditation. Rather than going off physically for a few days a year, we come daily into God's presence. Because we are learning to "pray without ceasing," by using our centering prayer day and night, we can become like the ark of the covenant that is carried into the world—a living, walking, working vessel of the glory of God. Our gracious God will never leave us, never forsake us. We are safe to live, to work, and to minister, carrying the lightest of burdens, the tabernacle of the living God.

Perhaps using the analogy of "mountain to plain" in speaking of the transfer from "prayer-life" to "world-life" is really not as good as thinking of ourselves being "decompressed" after a deep-sea dive. Divers come to the surface of the sea after a suitable period in each water depth because to emerge suddenly from the ocean floor would be to place their bodies in grave physical danger.

Likewise, we must "decompress" when we have been in deep communion in the "throne room." Saying the Lord's Prayer at the end of each meditation time helps; its beginning—"*Our* Father"—reminds us that God's plan is taking form in a world where Christianity not only involves a solitary relationship with God but also is something to be practiced in a corporate body in which we bear each other's burdens.

The rest of our Christian activity keeps our compression and decompression levels at the correct rate. We spend daily time in prayers of intercession, Bible study, vocal praise, and thanksgiving. Time is used regularly for worship and other services at our churches; and we are necessarily ready and active in our service to others. Meanwhile, we keep the centering prayer "running."

These are all part of the "manna" that must be gathered daily and hourly and weekly, a bread that cannot be saved or stored. We must gather it daily, just as the Israelites did, or our life in Christ will wither from loss of nourishment.

Soon our contemplative life will show. "You're different," a friend may say. Our impulses will have new, more spiritual qualities about them, and eventually others will want to know how we have such an intimate relationship with Christ. Such peace will surpass understanding by the modern world.

Several years ago I had surgery to correct a deviated septum and to straighten a previously broken nose. The doctor gave me a local anesthetic but also hooked me to an intravenous unit that could be activated to give me additional relief from pain or anxiety or even let me go to sleep for a while if necessary.

After a few moments he asked, "Are you always this calm?"

"I'm not in any pain," I told him. We repeated this conversation several times and also chatted about football teams and politics while he broke my nose in four places.

Finally he stopped. "You're the most peaceful woman I've ever met in my life. I've never had a patient with more extensive nose surgery, but everyone else has always wanted something for pain or anxiety. I want to know what you do."

I looked at him, knowing he was a Christian and knowing he had taken his premed work at a well-known church college.

"I pray," I told him, and tears came to his eyes. We spent the rest of surgery—after he had removed the IV from my arm, saying it was obvious that I didn't need it—talking about the deeper life with Jesus Christ.

Sometimes we are called to act quickly in God's name for the survival or salvation of another. Those who are able to use a centering prayer twenty-four hours a day find it easier, not harder, to emerge from sleep at 3 A.M. and speak to a suicidal person, or to make a snap decision in daylight to be God's witness. If we are truly centered, truly in perfect contact with God, we aren't off on an unrealistic emotional experience and we can return rapidly to the person or situation touching the hem of our garment, asking for help.

By the same token, the contemplative Christian is less likely to rush in where angels fear to tread. Running ahead of the

Lord seems to be a common error in the church; people *decide* that they are called to act, to speak, to "step out on faith" (which often means doing something risky in business and asking God to bless it afterwards).

But the centered man or woman, accustomed to nonrational, nonactive silence, is more deliberate. As the epistle writer James said,

> Each of you must be quick to listen, slow to speak, and slow to be angry. For a man's anger cannot promote the justice of God. Away then with all that is sordid, and the malice that hurries to excess, and quietly accept the message planted in your hearts, which can bring you salvation (James 1:19-21,NEB).

That "message planted in your hearts" is enhanced, enriched, and manifested through refreshing prayers of contemplation. The meditative Christian usually begins to speak less and to listen more; to seek the inner voice, which comes from God, and not add his or her own voice to the clamor of the world.

It is not always easy, however. Once, when teaching a class of Christian writers how to write about prayer, I told them, "I tend to think of my daily life as an interruption to my prayers." Later I realized that much of the time this is true; and that means I have to fight a tendency toward impatience with what I consider to be trivial.

Nothing in the life of a Christian is trivial. "God does not make mistakes," said Betsie Ten Boom to her sister Corrie, when they found themselves in a louse-infested dormitory at the forced-labor camp. Indeed, it turned out that Corrie and Betsie were able to continue ministering and leading Bible studies in that dormitory because the Nazi guards wanted to avoid the lice and so did not interfere. Those of us who seek God's face are required to remember that God may send strange signals into our lives. We impatiently brush off a person whose attentions or needs make us feel resentful and discover later that it was Christ we met on the road that day.

Remembering Christ's charge to "be perfect, even as our Father in heaven is perfect" calls up the corrected impulse.

Impatience submitted to prayer is transformed into eagerness for God. Anger turns to a thirst for justice, lust to love, and judgmentalism to scrupulousness about one's own life. Prayer is the laboratory where Christ works his water-to-wine miracles in our lives. Then, and only then, are we fit for the marketplace or for full-time Christian service.

There are many ways in which we can keep in touch with our own centering prayer. One man I know drives a school bus and is on the road much of the day. He trained himself to remember his brief prayer-words whenever he saw the colors red or green; now, every traffic intersection is a compelling call to prayer in the heart of this dedicated Christian.

Another young woman had a colicky baby that cried about eighteen hours a day. She frankly began to meditate in hopes that she could calm her shattered nerves, and she taught herself to say her centering prayer whenever she heard a baby cry. Today, her child is strong and calm, and she is one of the most spiritually mature women I have ever met.

It is important to remember that when we call on God, or even use God's name in a sentence or prayer, we are not using a mere word. God's name is indeed just that; a name.

It is this awareness of naming, this constant sense of the holy, that keeps our repetitions from being vain and our daily lives more like our prayer lives. We move in Christ, in the power of his love and being, as a fish swims and feeds and breathes in the water around him. If fish could speak, they might not have a word for "wet." Water would simply be there, as the source of all life.

So it is with God's holiness. We live in it, breathe it, drink it. The Holy Spirit pours glorification of Christ into our whole universe, and sometimes we think that because it is all about us, holiness is not existent. We don't call up the Holy Spirit with our prayers; the Spirit is always present as a member of the Godhead. When we meditate, we simply put ourselves in touch with what *is*—just as though the swimming fish could, suddenly, see and be aware of water. Thus, the trip back from the delight of contemplative prayer isn't so far, after all—only as far as one second to the next.

At the beginning of this chapter, we looked at God's Word to the Israelites on Mount Sinai (or Mount Horeb). There is another mountain that now needs our attention.

> Six days later Jesus took Peter, James, and John the brother of James, and led them up a high mountain where they were alone; and in their presence he was transfigured; his face shone like the sun and his clothes became white as the light (Matthew 17:1-3, NEB).

The story of all that happened on the mount of the transfiguration is part of another book. What is important to us today is the question "Who changed?"

Did Jesus suddenly *become* what they saw on the mountain, or did they actually *see* him for the first time? One would suspect that our Greek Orthodox brothers and sisters are right when they claim that it was not the visage of Christ which changed but the perception of the three disciples.

After this experience, the disciples were changed. On their way down from the mountain they asked about Elijah. Jesus answered them, saying rather cryptically that Elijah had come and that the world had not recognized him but had worked its will upon him. Immediately the disciples understood that he meant John the Baptist.

Amazing! Six days earlier, they had not been able to answer (except for Peter) the question "Who do men say that I am?" Now they could decode the most enigmatic of Jesus' remarks. Something had changed, and the biblical account of the way down the mountain shows it to us.

Thus, we change. Once having even glimpsed the glory of our Savior, once having perceived through sense or spirit that this, indeed, is the victor King, we are different. We are, as in Paul's words, transformed from glory to glory, and our understanding and love begin to blossom.

The Christ-centered life is not an easy life. There is currently a rash of books and speakers who ask us to believe that God intends for us all to be rich, slender, and healthy, with good teeth and naturally curly hair. Enemies melt before our eyes, cancers disappear, and money drops from nowhere.

There is no such life on earth. There are healings that astonish the scientific mind, changes in the attitudes of our enemies, and many moments when it is apparent that God has chosen to intervene in our lives. But we are also promised tribulation as long as we are in the world, and it becomes clear to anyone who leaps into the cloud of unknowing to see the transfigured Christ that the world is still fallen, still groaning in travail, and still not an easy place for a covenanted Christian to live. If we really follow Christ, the mountaintop we seek most diligently will be the one with the cross on top.

Glossary of Terms

Centering prayer: a word or phrase used as the focus of daily meditation periods and as a constant interior phrase to bring the person into a ceaseless relationship of prayer.

Contemplation: a stage of prayer achieved by pursuing meditation or centering prayer until the prayer itself stops, the sense of self disappears, and God is found in the silence.

Contemplative: a life-style devoted to constant inner prayer; people who devote their lives to prayer are often called "contemplatives."

Meditation: a kind of prayer beyond traditional petition or thanksgiving in which the mind and body are centered on one thought or aspect of God. This is sometimes called "mental prayer."

Union: a state of prayer in which the individual is completely absorbed by the presence of God and is one with God.

Notes

Chapter 2

[1] William Johnston, ed., *The Cloud of Unknowing and the Book of Privy Counselling* (Garden City, N.Y.: Doubleday & Co., Inc., Image Books, 1973), p. 48.

[2] *Ibid.*, p. 97.

[3] *The Way of the Pilgrim,* trans. R. M. French (New York: The Seabury Press, Crossroads Books, 1965), p. 12. For further study of this prayer see Per-Olaf Sjogren, *The Jesus Prayer,* trans. Sydney Linton (Philadelphia: Fortress Press, 1975), American edition. Also see Arthur Vogel, *The Jesus Prayer for Today* (New York: Paulist Press, 1982).

[4] Ron DelBene and Herb Montgomery, *The Breath of Life: A Simple Way to Pray* (Minneapolis: Winston Press, Inc., 1981).

[5] Quoted in William McNamara, *Mystical Passion: Spirituality for a Bored Society* (New York: Paulist Press, 1977), p. 9.

[6] Johnston, *op.cit.*, p. 45.

[7] Carolyn Rhea, *My Heart Kneels, Too* (New York: Grosset & Dunlap, Inc., 1968), p. 28.

[8] A. W. Tozer, *The Pursuit of God* (Beaverlodge, Alberta, Canada: Horizon House, 1976), p. 81.

Chapter 3

[1] A. W. Tozer, *The Pursuit of God* (Beaverlodge, Alberta, Canada: Horizon House, 1976), pp. 81-82.

Chapter 4

[1] Morton Kelsey, *Dreams: A Way to Listen to God* (New York: Paulist Press, 1978), p. 79.

[2] Quoted in *ibid.*, p. 74.

[3] Catherine Marshall, *Something More* (Carmel, N. Y.: Guidepost Associates, Inc., 1974), p. 88.

Chapter 5

[1] C. S. Lewis, *Mere Christianity* (New York: Macmillan, Inc., 1943, 1970), p. 167.
[2] Quoted in William McNamara, *Mystical Passion: Spirituality for a Bored Society* (New York: Paulist Press, 1977), p. 72.

Chapter 8

[1] From C. S. Lewis, *The Last Battle* (New York: Macmillan, Inc., 1969).
[2] Teresa of Avila, *Autobiography*, trans. E. Allison Peers (Garden City, N. Y.: Doubleday & Co., Inc., Image Books, 1960). Teresa's four ways of watering are the basis for most of the chapters.
[3] Dietrich Bonhoeffer, *The Cost of Discipleship* (New York: Macmillan, Inc., 1963), p. 161.

Chapter 9

[1] William McNamara, *Mystical Passion: Spirituality for a Bored Society* (New York: Paulist Press, 1977), p. 72.